ART SONG

ART SONG

The Marriage of Music and Poetry

by

Barbara Meister

Hollowbrook Publishing
Durango, Colorado

Published in 1992 by Hollowbrook Publishing, a division of Hollowbrook Communications, Inc.,

Library of Congress Cataloging in Publication Data:

Meister, Barbara, 1932-
    Art song : the marriage of music and poetry / by Barbara
    Meister
        p.   cm.
    Includes bibliographical references
    ISBN 0-89341-635-5
    1. Songs--Analysis, appreciation.   2. Music and literature.
I. Title
MT110,M44   1991
782.42168'09--do20   *91-12788*
                                                      CIP
                                                      MN

Printed in U.S.A.

To Caitlin, Claudia, Arel,
Jessica, Asher, and Dillon

ACKNOWLEDGEMENTS

Several very learned and very busy people have helped me with this study, and I should like to thank them: first Dr. Rodney Jilg for his thought-provoking comments on the structure and content of the Copland-Dickinson chapter; second, Suzanne Osborne for her erudite and sensitive readings of the German poems; and finally Victor Trasoff and Ursula Pfeffer for their part in the editing and re-editing of the manuscript.

NOTE TO THE READER

It is the author's hope that this study will prove of interest to devotees of poetry per se, as well as to those who enjoy the music that has been created around it. For this reason, and at the risk of boring those steeped in one or both art forms, any technical terms which might not be familiar to all have been defined in the text.

Similarly, for the convenience of all readers, even the simplest phrases in a foreign language have been translated.

No attempt has been made to make the chapters symmetrical: composers whose biographies are common knowledge are merely identified, while lesser-known figures are introduced at some length. The same unequal treatment has been given to periods and styles.

TABLE OF CONTENTS

INTRODUCTION   xiii

I.   MOZART   1
Das Veilchen— GOETHE

II.   FRANZ SCHUBERT   9
Erlkönig— GOETHE
Gretchen am Spinnrade— GOETHE
Ganymed— GOETHE
Der Tod und das Mädchen— CLAUDIUS
Ständchen— RELLSTAB
Der Doppelgänger— HEINE

III. ROBERT SCHUMANM   49
Frauenliebe und -leben— CHAMISSO

IV. BRAHMS   76
Die Mainacht— HÖLTY
Das Vergebliches Ständchen— ANON
Mädchenlied— HEYSE

V.   HUGO WOLF   93
Das Verlassene Mägdlein— MÖRIKE
Begegnung— MÖRIKE

VI. RICHARD STRAUSS   106
Ständchen— VON SCHACK

VII. HENRI DUPARC   111
Phidylé— LECONTE DE LISLE

VIII. CLAUDE DEBUSSY   120
Colloque sentimental— VERLAINE
Harmonie du soir— BAUDELAIRE

Chansons de Bilitis— LOUŸS
  La Flûte De Pan
  La Chevelure
  Le Tombeau des Naiades

IX. GABRIEL FAURÉ   153
Poème d'un jour— GRANDMOUGIN
  Rencontre
  Toujours
  Adieu

X. GEORGES AURIC   167
Album— RADIGUET
  Album
  Bateau
  Domino
  Filet a pàpillons
  Mallarmé
  Hirondelle
  Escarpin

XI. AARON COPLAND   189
Twelve Poems of EMILY DICKINSON

BIBLIOGRAPHY   225

INTRODUCTION

The principal elements of music are melody, rhythm and harmony. Since poetry depends on rhythmic patterns, metric accents and tempo variations, and since when read aloud or vocally imagined it has a degree of melodic content caused by the rising and falling pitch levels of the human voice, the only characteristic of music not found in poetry is harmony, the last of music's elements to develop and the only one not found in all forms of music.

The most salient characteristic of all linguistic endeavor, be it oral or written, prose or poetry, not intrinsic to musical thought is referentiality. No note or combination of notes can properly be said to "mean" anything other than itself, no note or combination of notes is a sign accepted by a large group of listeners as pointing to some real or imagined object in the way in which a word is so accepted.

This must in no way be taken to indicate that music itself has no meaning. There are indeed two types of musical meaning, which can and almost always do overlap: the structural and the expressive. If a composition is written in the key of C major, the note C functions as the note around which all others gravitate; that so-called tonic note provides a home base, a point of reference, a beginning and an end to the scale from which the melody is derived, a root note for the chord on which the harmony is based. That same note, whose "meaning" as function is a purely musical one, can have emotive power as well—one will probably have a sense of completion or arrival on hearing it at the end of a phrase, for example—and both these kinds of meanings must be considered when music exists of and for itself as well as when it is used in combination with poetry. Music and poetry have been defined as sister arts which exemplify "the shaped flow of time."[1] Like close members of any family, they are sometimes more and sometimes less compatible. According to James Winn they "begin together, and the frequent separations in their history lead to equally frequent reconciliations."[2] All the evidence we have indicates that they were inseparable in ancient Greece and virtually tied to one another in the songs of the medieval troubadours. In the Baroque era, as music grew more complex, the relationship of music and poetry became more problematic. The increased independence of instrumental writing as well as the development of polyphony in vocal and instrumental music made comprehension of any words set to music difficult if not impossible, and it is an interesting paradox that in this manifestly Christian era, when the Word was paramount, the music of the majestic choral works of Palestrina, Monteverdi, Handel and Bach, admittedly among the greatest achievements of the Baroque period, obscured the very texts they were intended to glorify.

Early in the seventeenth century, while the Baroque style of composition was still maturing—Bach and Handel, two of the world's greatest masters of choral polyphony, were not born until 1685—a reaction set in against polyphony in vocal music. The place was Florence and the result was a new form of opera based on one single vocal line with minimum accompaniment. The Florentine composers were reflecting the Renaissance aesthetic, honoring Greek ideals as they understood them by placing the music at the service of the words. Expressive recitative was part of the Florentine idiom, for this semi-declamatory style promises optimum comprehensibility of the words.

Songs of the Classical era, the age of Haydn, Mozart and early Beethoven, owe more to the Florentine tradition than to the high Baroque, and it is not until the works of Franz Schubert (1797-1828) that the words and music of a vocal composition once again came to have equal status in the eyes of a European composer. In fact, Schubert's first published works, his Opus 1 (*Der Erlkönig*) and Opus 2 (*Gretchen am Spinnrade*) changed the concept of lieder, or art song, for the musician, for in those two compositions Schubert took what he felt to be one principal characteristic of the text—the galloping horse in the first, the spinning wheel in the second—and gave musical expression to these elements exclusively in the piano part. In these songs the singer and the pianist have two different tasks to perform; neither is in the service of the other, both are in the service of the overall message of the song.

In a song with a fully realized accompaniment, says Edward Cone, the composer's 'voice' is more extensive than the poem's 'persona', for the vocal part is not the whole story.[3] The composer of an art song speaks with a double voice through a musical persona that assumes a double guise, continues Mr. Cone. This has become true only since the songs of Franz Schubert.

Virtually every music lover claims to feel an emotional response, no matter how vague or idiosyncratic, to music. In the majority of cases this response has little to do with a technical knowledge of musical theory. Leonard Meyer, in his brilliant *Emotion and Meaning in Music* (University of Chicago Press, 1956), systematically tackles the question of why listeners have this response to music, whether or not it is combined with poetry. Citing evidence for the existence of "undifferentiated emotions" and "emotional states much more subtle and varied than are the few crude and standardized words we use to denote them" (pp. 8-10), Meyer gives specific instances of the revelation of these "states of soul" by music. "Expectation is always ahead of the music," he writes, "creating a background of diffuse tension against which particular delays articulate the affective curve and create meaning...generalized aesthetic tension is shaped and particularized in the course of listening" (pp. 59-60).

Over the course of the history of Western civilization, many responses to music have become quasi-automatic: dissonance, for example, has become synonymous with tension, and consonance with release and repose; the former implies deviance and movement, the latter stability and normality. (As a dissonance becomes familiar and overworked, it gradually takes on the effect of a consonance, so that the history of music has been one of the gradual introduction and acceptance of former dissonances as stable combinations, and the constant addition of new, harsher sounds to the legitimate vocabulary of harmony.) In similar fashion the minor mode has long been associated with melancholia while the major tonalities are usually used to display light- hearted pleasure; rapid tempi have always implied animation or agitation while slower movement suggests meditation or sorrow. There are other, more particular connotations, learned from repeated usage over long periods of time, such as the associations of the pentatonic scale, the timbre of the flute and the gentle rocking of 6/8 time with the pastoral mode, the interpretation of a descending 'down-up' two-note phrase as a sigh, the equating of a long trill with expectation, the sounding of a triadic trumpet call to arouse patriotic or martial sentiment, the use of Ecclesiastical modes to suggest archaisms, and so forth. All these conditioned responses demonstrate the tendency in most cultures to associate musical with extramusical experience.[5] In short, "music connotes...rich realms of experience...consolidated into a single connotative complex."[6]

The most important aspect of music's contribution to the emotional life of the listener may very well be the way in which it presents feelings "directly to our understanding...without the scaffolding of an occasion wherein they figure";[7] it adds an element to the words which their very specificity, their referentiality, prohibits them from imparting. Thus text and setting are complementary, with music presenting emotional analogues in an abstract manner and language making specific the occasions for the emotions exposed.

An interesting example, albeit a fictional one, of the emotive power the interaction of voice and instrumental music can exert occurs in Thomas Mann's novel *Doctor Faustus*. Towards the end of the story the author describes an imaginary composition written by his hero, Adrian Leverkühn, in which "a singular interchange" takes place between the orchestra and the chorus: "Chorus and orchestra are here not clearly separated from each other as symbols of the human and the material world; they merge into each other, the chorus is 'instrumentalized,' the orchestra as it were 'vocalized,' to that degree and to that end that the boundary between man and thing seems shifted: ...there is about it something oppressive, dangerous, malignant...the muted trumpet suggests a grotesque vox humana..."[8] Even more telling than this perverse exchange is Leverkühn's use of howling and shrieking glissandi, which makes of this section of *Apocalypse*, as the piece is called, a reversion to the most primitive state of inchoate musical expression. The most elemental step in the creation of music as an artistic rather than a merely instinctive expression of human emotions is the achievement of definite and individual pitch levels or notes; this rudimentary step is vitiated by Leverkühn's glissando-ridden music, which thus becomes a barbaric, atavistic analogue for the rise of Nazism in the Germany of the 1930's.

In an art song the poetic text predates the music. Since the composer has an unlimited choice of texts, it seems axiomatic that something about the specific poem chosen must have inspired the composer to attempt to convey its meaning in musical terms. This would seem to indicate that the text should be of primary importance in the finished product, and many characteristics of art song indicate that it is. Few art songs, for instance, have the kind of vocal display, common in operatic arias, that would make it impossible to understand the words; seldom is the piano accompaniment (unfortunate term, since so much of the meaning and emotive content is provided by the piano part) allowed to drown out the vocal line, as the orchestra can hardly help doing in much grand opera. Even the tessitura is kept within reasonable bounds by most art song composers, again in the interests of intelligibility of the words. And yet, for many serious analysts of art song, the poetic text is, by "the principle of assimilation," incorporated into the musical matrix, becoming an element of the music in the same way that rhythm, harmony and melody are elements of it.[9] Susanne Langer agrees with Sir Donald Francis Tovey that vocal music without words, such as Vaughn-Williams' *Vocalise* or Debussy's *Sirènes*, "thrusts all instruments aside...only to disappoint the expectation of human speech.[10] Nevertheless, she insists that the poem is necessarily "swallowed" by the music as the poetic idea is transformed into a musical one.

Lawrence Kramer feels that "the relationship between poetry and music in song is implicitly agonic, the song becoming a 'new creation' only because it is a decreation. The music appropriates the poem by contending with it, phonetically, dramatically and semantically, and the contest is what most drives and shapes the song."[11]

Some poets have feared an obliteration of their texts in musical settings, but disagreement may be found among poets and theorists alike. For George Steiner, for example, a song setting is "an act of interpretive restatement in which the verbal sign system is critically illuminated...or misconstrued by a non-verbal sign system with its own highly formal syntax...[The song is] a construct in which the original and its 'translation' coexist in active simultaneity."[12] In Jacques Barzun's opinion, "...music begins to speak to us at the point where words stop...",[13] and composer Mario Castelnuovo-Tedesco hopes in his own song settings "to stamp [the poems] with the authentic and therefore undetachable seal of melody, give utterance to the music that is latent within them,...and to discover their real source in the emotions that brought them into being."[14]

The interesting word in the Castelnuovo-Tedesco statement is "undetachable," for it is true that once a poem has been learned to the accompaniment of a suitable melody, it becomes almost impossible to think of the former without the latter. In fact, it is often a tune that makes it possible to memorize a verbal passage, as the minstrels of old well knew.

The theory of synaesthesia holds that correspondences among the senses, reflected in comparable correspondences among the arts, make it possible to translate images and moods from one medium into another. In the composite aesthetic form known as art song it is not so much a question of translating words into music as it is of creating a new vehicle capable of expressing the content of the poetry as it is filtered through the emotions, intelligence and aesthetic preferences of the composer. Abstract discussions of the interaction of music and poetry such as those touched upon in the preceding pages are endlessly fascinating to the lover of art song, but it seems to this listener and performer that descriptions of what actually happens in specific examples of the genre are at least as much to the point. It is therefore the aim of this study to demonstrate, through analyses of some of the most familiar and best loved songs in the recital repertoire—as well as several rarely encountered personal favorites—how a composer is able to put the expressive content of the text he selects into musical terms, and how he is often able thereby to intensify and clarify the poet's thoughts, expressing in harmony, melody and rhythm the images partly concealed and partly revealed by the words themselves.

Notes to Introduction

1. Kramer, Lawrence, *Music and Poetry, The Nineteenth Century and After* (University of California Press, 1984) p. 241.
2. Winn, James Anderson, *Unsuspected Eloquence* (Yale University Press, 1981) p. 1.
3. Cone, Edward, *The Composer's Voice* (University of California Press, 1974) pp. 10-11.

4. Hospers, John, *Meaning and Truth in the Arts* (University of North Carolina, 1946) p. 230

5. Meyer, pp. 259-262

6. Meyer, pp. 265

7. Langer, Susanne, *Philosophy in a New Key* (Harvard University Press, 1957) p. 222.

8. Mann, Thomas, *Doctor Faustus* (New York: Knopf, 1963) p. 375.

9. Langer, Susanne, *Feeling and Form* (New York: Charles Scribner's Sons, 1953) p. 164.

10. Tovey, Sir Donald Francis, *Essays in Musical Analysis. Volume V. Vocal Music* (Oxford University Press, 1937) p. 1.

11. Kramer, p. 127

12. Steiner, George, *After Babel* (Oxford University Press, 1975) p. 419.

13. Barzun, Jacques, "Music into Words," *Score* #10, December 1954, pp. 50-65.

14. Castelnuovo-Tedesco, Mario, "Music and Poetry," *Musical Quarterly* XXX, pp. 102-111.

CHAPTER I

MOZART

DAS VEILCHEN   Goethe

When André Gide was asked who, in his opinion, was the greatest French poet of all time, he replied "Victor Hugo, hélas!" which is why, so the story goes, one occasionally hears that towering nineteenth-century poet, novelist and dramatist ruefully referred to as "M. Hélas." No equivalent "ach!" would be likely to accompany the reply to such a question asked in German, for the mastery of Johann Wolfgang von Goethe (1749-1832) goes undisputed and unregretted in the history of German literature.

Despite the estimable poetry of Martin Opitz (1597-1639), Christian Gellert (1715-1769), Friedrich Klopstock (1724-1803) and others, and above all the brilliant criticism of Gotthold Lessing (1729-1781), it was Goethe whose work brought German poetry, drama and fiction to the attention of the educated European community. In his long, productive career Goethe epitomized one phase of literature after another, developing, absorbing and then bringing to a peak the *Aufklärung* (Enlightenment), the *Sturm und Drang* (Storm and Stress) period and the *Klassiche* (Classical) era. The suicide of the protagonist of his novel *The Sorrows of Young Werther* (1774) was blamed for a rash of similar deaths all over the continent, as young men copied not only Werther's costume but the tragic resolution to his story.

Goethe's poems and plays have been translated and set to music in all major European languages. For decades Gounod's version of Goethe's *Faust* was France's best loved opera, and "Kennst du das Land," one of Mignon's songs in his novel *Wilhelm Meister*, may very well be the text with the largest number of settings in the entire Lieder repertoire (according to one source there are over 3000 songs based on Goethe poems).[1]

"Das Veilchen," the song analyzed here and the only Goethe text

used by Mozart, was originally part of a Singspiel (a musical play
or an opera with spoken dialogue) called *Erwin and Elvira* which
was written by Goethe in 1773. According to the plot, Erwin
writes the poem for Elvira, who has hitherto scorned his love, to
sing. When she realizes that the sad little ballad refers to their
own unhappy affair, her heart is softened and she accepts the poet,
indicating that whatever its merits or lack thereof in the
contemporary reader's eyes, in its own world the poem was seen
as successful. (Were Gilbert and Sullivan parodying this scene in
Koko's wonderful "Tit-Willow" song in *The Mikado*?)

DAS VEILCHEN

Ein Veilchen auf der Wiese stand
Gebückt in sich und unbekannt:
Es war ein herzig's Veilchen!
Da kam ein' junge Schäferin
Mit leichtem Schritt und munterm Sinn
Daher, daher,
Die Wiese her und sang.

"Ach!" denkt das Veilchen, "wär' ich nur
Die schönste Blume der Natur,
Ach! nur ein kleines Weilchen,
Bis mich das Liebchen abgepflückt
Und an dem Busen matt gedrückt,
Ach nur, ach nur,
Ein Viertelstündchen lang!"

Ach, aber ach! das Mädchen kam
Und nicht in Acht das Veilchen nahm,
Ertrat's das arme Veilchen.
Und sank und starb und freut'sich noch:
"Und sterb' ich denn, so sterb' ich doch
Durch sie, durch sie,
Zu ihren Füssen doch!"

THE VIOLET

A violet on the meadow stood
Head bowed down and unknown:
It was a lovely violet!
A young shepherdess came
With a dainty step and carefree spirit
Hither, hither,
Through the meadow singing.

Ah, thinks the violet. If only I were
The loveliest flower of nature,
Oh, only for a little while,
Until the little darling could pluck me
And press me to her bosom.
Ah, only, ah only
For a little quarter of an hour!

Oh, but oh! The maiden came
And did not notice the violet,
Stepped on the poor violet.
It sank and died and rejoiced even so:
"For then I die indeed
Through her, through her,
Beneath her feet."

"Das Veilchen" and *The Sorrows of Young Werther* were written at the same time, but how different are their stories and their styles! Perhaps Goethe was amusing himself with the Singspiel as relief from the weighty work of the novel, for it is hard to believe that the reader is meant to take either the overall plot of *Erwin and Elvira* or the violet's tale within it very seriously. In this distancing of the reader from the emotions apparently described by the poem one finds a major characteristic of the style known as Rococo, which was a light-hearted offshoot of the rationalistic *Aufklärung* noted as well for its "conscious and deliberately chosen element of play" as well as for its fanciful metric freedom.[2]

The Rococo aura of "Das Veilchen" is created by many specific and definable elements. First, we might cite the choice of a "Veilchen," with its built-in diminutive ending and its connotations of fragility, timidity and miniature size, to represent the male protagonist, followed by the use of "Liebchen," another word with a normally diminutive ending, for the term of endearment the violet uses for the shepherdess. Then there are the added "chens" which make of the more common *eine Weile "ein kleines Weilchen"* (a *little little* while) and of *eine Viertelstunde "ein Viertelstundchen,"* a *little* quarter of an hour. There is no doubt that we are to think small! Added to all this diminution are the pastoral allusions which evoke Watteau-like landscapes of silk-and-satin garbed shepherds and shepherdesses exchanging amorous glances while their sheep graze. Above all is the eager joy, admittedly somewhat contradicted by the text's seven pitiful *ach's*, with which the hero embraces his literally crushing fate. There is certainly a gentle irony at work here.

The rhyme scheme of "Das Veilchen," with its complex mixture of matched and unmatched endsounds and its interplay between strophes, is technically well-suited to its Rococo vocabulary. Each of the stanzas consists of seven lines, in itself an unusual arrangement. The first two strophes have end-sounds in an A/A/B/C/C/D/E pattern, with the last syllables of the final lines creating a rhyme ("sang"/"lang"); the pattern of the last strophe is A/A/B/C/C/D/C, giving a self-contained final rhyme. The lines are of uneven length, ranging from eight to four syllables, with freely varied stress patterns.

Mozart wrote his first Singspiel, a religious work called *Die Schuldigkeit des ersten Gebotes,* when he was eleven years old and his last, *Die Zauberflöte,* five months before his death. Obviously the form, with its opportunities for characterization, drama, comedy, passion, lyricism and even slapstick buffoonery, and its easy acceptance of Italianate arias, Germanic folk-songs, accompanied recitative and spoken dialogue, appealed to him all his life, and it is safe to say that he brought the form to its highest peak. Perhaps this affinity for Singspiel has something to do with the success of Mozart's setting of "Das Veilchen," regarded by many as the best of the master's 36 songs for solo voice and piano accompaniment.

If one did not know that Goethe's "Das Veilchen" was part of a larger work, the poem would seem a satisfactory entity in itself, and so Mozart treats it, in fact making of the little verse narrative a sort of miniature opera. A seven-bar piano- prelude introduces the through-composed song's principal melodic line and then comes to a full cadential close before the voice enters (Ex. I).

Ex. I

Until the key word "Veilchen" the setting is syllabic—one note for each syllable of text—so the two-note phrase on the first syllable of that all-important word imparts considerable emphasis to it. The downward direction of those two notes, while not yet particularly evocative, hints at future sighing (Ex II).

Ex. II

Ex. III

The shepherdess's light, dainty steps are represented musically by staccato sixteenth notes in the accompaniment and airy spaces between the rhythmically uneven notes in the melodic line; her song is represented by legato running notes in both parts (Ex. III). The piano interlude separating the first two strophes continues the musical imagery associated with this charming young lady.

Suddenly, at the second stanza's opening "ach!" where the poem shifts from descriptions of the sweet shepherdess to a depiction of the violet's anguish, Mozart moves from the major to the minor mode and from gaily tripping sixteenth-notes to heavy eighth-note chords. The dominant-seventh chord under "Blumen" prepares us for a modulation to B flat major as the violet wishes he were the fairest flower in all nature. Carried along by this wishful thinking, the melody and ornamental turns in the accompaniment move the song happily along until the next "ach," where the violet limits his obviously unattainable wish to a mere *little* quarter of an hour. These pathetic phrases underlying diminished and minor harmonies bode future sorrow, despite the fact that the second strophe, like the first, ends on a D major (the dominant) chord. It is interesting to note how the two approaches to this feminine close—the first from the standard A seven, the second from what may be seen as an altered C minor—affect the impact of the D major resolution.

The piano interlude between the second and third strophes consists of one measure of fortissimo chords. A dramatic pause in the accompaniment after "Ach, aber ach!" makes the rising vocal line more ominous than it would otherwise be, and this feeling of trouble-to-come is reinforced by the piano's repetition of the singer's phrase (Ex. IV).

Ex. IV

The climactic verse "und nicht in acht das Veilchen nahm" is sung in dramatic recitative style, with only a diminished chord under "nahm" to support the vocal line, after which "ertrat," the somewhat unusual term for "trampled" ("zertrat" is more common) is also sung without accompaniment. Powerful chords ending in a diminished harmony, a sure signal of distress in Mozart's vocabulary, underscore the rising melodic line of "das arme Veilchen," the high point of the song in terms of intensity, if not in actual pitch. After a long pause the voice continues to tell the plaintive story, with sobbing or at least sighing downward two-note phrases on the single syllables "sank" and "starb." Melody and accompaniment come to a conventional full close at the end of Goethe's final line, "zu ihren Füßen doch," but Mozart opts to write a coda, adding "Das arme Veilchen! / es war ein herzigs Veilchen" to the text so that the music can come to yet another full close (Ex. V).

Ex. V

Throughout his setting of "Das Veilchen" Mozart captures and reinforces Goethe's gently teasing mood, indicating by the *allegretto* tempo marking, the onomatopoeic staccato accompaniment for the shepherdess's steps, the musical emphasis on the "achs," the exaggerated drama of the recitative passages, and above all the falling minor third of the coda's "Das arme Veilchen," that he enjoyed and deliberately chose to recreate the Rococo playfulness of the original text.

Notes to Chapter I

1. Elaine Brody and Robert A. Fowkes, *The German Lied and its Poetry* (N.Y.U. Press, 1971) p. 13.
2. Alan Menhennet, Order and Freedom: *Literature and Society in Germany from 1790 to 1805* (New York: Basic Books, 1973) p. 89.

CHAPTER II

FRANZ SCHUBERT

ERLKÖNIG   Goethe

If Goethe's "Das Veilchen" represents the benign tapering-off of severe, erudite, Enlightenment rationality into the more playful, witty Rococo, his feverish "Erlkönig" brings us to the height of *Sturm und Drang*, by far the more violent reaction to the older *Aufklärung* style.

Written in 1782, while Goethe was in service at the Weimar court of Duke Karl August, "Erlkönig" is more or less contemporary with "An den Mond," "Der Fischer," "Kennst du das Land" and other "highwater marks of [his] lyric genius."[1] The intensity of his lyric outpouring from let us say 1775 to 1785 is partially attributable to the new *zeitgeist*, a vague but strong feeling championed by Johann Gottfried Herder (1744-1803), Johann Friedrich Schiller (1759-1805), Friedrich Müller (1749-1825), Ludwig Christoph Hölty (1748-1776) and others. (The seeds of this movement may be found even earlier, in the work of Friedrich Gottlieb Klopstock, 1724-1803.) The tendency of the movement was to assert that the self must be liberated from the constraints of reason and bourgeois morality for the attainment of true freedom.[2] (This was evidently the more personal, apolitical German response to the spirit of revolution rampant in France and the American Colonies at this time.) An equally strong contributing factor to his avid participation in the anti-rationalist style was undoubtedly Goethe's own turbulent love-life during this decade, which saw the end of his affair with Charlotte Buff, the beginning and end of his love for Charlotte von Stein, and several other stormy entanglements.

Goethe's "Erlkönig" (there are other versions of the old legend) rapidly became one of the best-known ballads in the German

language, and was soon appearing in anthologies all through
Europe. There were even countless parodies of the work, a
sure-fire measure of the magnitude of its fame. In a way, this
story of the battle among the mythical evil spirit known as the king
of the elves, the young boy he covets and the child's father, sums
up the *Sturm und Drang* artist's argument against the Enlightenment. Certainly the father has reason on his side: he knows that
there is no such thing as an Elfking, that his son is mistaking the
rustling of the dry leaves for the voice of a supernatural being, that
the crown and train the boy sees are bits of mist, and he is
undoubtedly right. Nevertheless, when they reach home after the
breathless ride, the boy is dead. Of natural causes? Of fright?
Who is to say? In any case, the poet, readers and the protagonists
themselves are meant to respond not to logical examination of the
facts as stated, but to the inherent expressive force of the imagery,
as indeed they do in this brilliant "evocation of mysterious
presences in nature."[3]

ERLKÖNIG

Wer reitet so spät durch Nacht und Wind?
Es ist der Vater mit seinem Kind:
er hat den Knaben wohl in dem Arm,
er faßt ihn sicher, er hält ihn warm.

"Mein Sohn, was birgst du so bang dein Gesicht?"
"Siehst, Vater, du den Erlkönig nicht?
den Erlenkönig mit Kron und Schweif?"
˜Mein Sohn, es ist ein Nebelstreif."

"Du liebes Kind, komm, geh mit mir!
gar schöne Spiele spiel ich mit dir;
manch bunte Blumen sind an dem Strand,
meine Mutter hat manch gülden Gewand."

"Mein Vater, mein Vater, und hörest du nicht,
was Erlenkönig mir leise verspricht?"
"Sei ruhig, bleibe ruhig, mein Kind:
in dürren Blättern säuselt der Wind."

"Willst, feiner Knabe, du mit mir gehn?
meine Töchter sollen dich warten schön;
meine Töchter führen den nächtlichen Reihn
und wiegen und tanzen und singen dich ein."

"Mein Vater, mein Vater, und siehst du nicht dort
Erlkönigs Töchter am düstern Ort?"
"Mein Sohn, mein Sohn, ich seh' es genau,
es scheinen die alten Weiden so grau."

"Ich liebe dich, mich reizt deine schöne Gestalt,
und bist du nicht willig, so brauch ich Gewalt."
"Mein Vater, mein Vater, jetzt faßt er mich an!
Erlkönig hat mir ein Leids getan!"

Dem Vater grauset's, er reitet geschwind,
er hält in Armen das ächzende Kind,
erreicht den Hof, mit Müh und Not;
in seinen Armen das Kind war tot.

THE ELFKING

Who rides so late through night and wind?
It is the father with his child.
He holds the lad in his arms,
He grasps him safely, he keeps him warm.

"My son, why do you so fearfully hide your face?"
"Father, do you not see the Elfking?
The Elfking with his crown and train?"
My son, it is a wisp of fog."

"You dear child, come, go with me!
I'll play wonderful games with you;
Many varicolored flowers are on the shore,
My mother has many a golden gown."

"My father, my father, don't you hear
What the Elfking softly promises me?"

"Be calm, stay calm, my child;
The wind is rustling in the dry leaves."

"Will you, fine youth, go with me?
My daughters shall wait on you nicely;
My daughters lead the nocturnal dance
And will rock, and dance and sing you to sleep."

"My father, my father, can you not yet see
The Elfking's daughters there in the darkness?"
"My son, my son, I see it exactly,
The old willows are shining there so grey."

"I love you, your fair form enchants me
And if you are not willing then I will use force."
"My father, my father, now he is grabbing me!
The Elfking has hurt me!"

The father is horrified, he rides swiftly,
He holds the moaning child in his arms;
With distress and urgency he reaches the courtyard;
In his arms the child was dead.

Goethe has given his ballad a rigid A/A B/B rhyme scheme,
with most lines end-stopped and accents on all final syllables (the
only possible *enjambement* is between the first two lines of the
sixth strophe, and a natural pause is really not out of place even
there). There are four strong beats to each line, with some
variation in the number of weak beats between accents, although
the iambic pattern predominates. It is easy to hear the rhythm of
a galloping horse in this persistent strong-weak, strong-weak,
strong-weak, strong-weak arrangement.

The ballad begins with a question, and further interrogatives are
used in all but the last two stanzas. From the first to the last line
the father holds the child in his arms, but the movement is from
what he sees as security despite the boy's questions ("er faßt ihn
sicher, er hält ihn warm") to the certainty of tragedy ("in seinen
Armen das Kind war tot"). In the second line of the second
strophe the unusual word order places emphasis on the "du"

(Father, don't *you* see the Elfking?); in the following line the poetic word "Schweif," with its possible translations of "train" or "tail" (as in the tail of a comet, perhaps) calls attention to itself. When the Elfking first speaks to the boy (Strophe III) it is in a commanding tone full of hard sounds and abrupt, single- syllable words ("Kind, komm, geh mit mir"), but in the following line the wily spirit switches to a whispering, insinuating style, which Goethe indicates with the soft sounds of "schöne, "Spiele,", "spiel" and "ich." The opening line of Strophe V has a word-order inversion focusing on the "du" similar to that in Strophe II ("Willst, feiner Knabe, du mit mir gehn?"), and the archaic "Reihn" in the third line of that stanza (it would be "Reigen" in modern German) adds to the "once-upon-a-time" aura. In keeping with the conventions of ballad form, most of "Erlkönig" is told in the present tense, making Goethe's two excursions into the past— "the Elfking *has hurt* me" in the last line of Strophe VII and "In his arms the boy *was* dead" at the end of the poem—all the more interesting.

Schubert's setting of "Erlkönig," one of many and evidently not Goethe's favorite, was composed in 1815 when Schubert was eighteen years old. It was published six years later as the composer's Opus I. In 1815 Schubert wrote 145 songs, thirty of them to texts by Goethe including some of those best known and most often performed ("Heidenröslein," "Erster Verlust," "Wanderers Nachtlied" and "Rastlose Liebe" are among them), but the "Erlkönig" is undoubtedly the outstanding song of his eighteenth year. ("Gretchen am Spinnrade," composed in October of 1814 and just as powerful a work, was published soon after "Erlkönig" as Opus II; "Schäfers Klagelied," "Erster Verlust," "Heidenröslein," "Rastlose Lieber," "König in Thule" and "Jäger's Abendlied" were other Schubert songs to Goethe texts published in 1821 as Opp. I-VIII. We need only note the reverse order of the publication of "Erlkönig" and "Gretchen" to be reminded that opus numbers are not much help in establishing the chronology of Schubert's enormous output.)

Many poets have utilized the dialogue form and many dialogue poems have been set to music, but seldom if ever has as complicated a scena as "Erlkönig," with its four distinct voices (nar-

rator, father, child and Elfking himself), tempted so many composers.   According to German scholar Dr. Herbert Zeman,
Schubert himself was not sure that one performer could do justice
to all the roles, so he staged "Erlkönig" as a mini-drama in which
he, his friend and supporter, Austrian baritone Johann Michael
Vogl, and a young lady whose name has been forgotten sang the
various parts (it is not clear who played the narrator).[4] The effect
of the song when performed "straight"—that is by one soloist—is
of course incomparable, nd Schubert may very well have been
having fun at his own expense with the staged version.

The great innovative aspect of "Erlkönig" was the establishing
of a musical analogue for one vital characteristic of the text and the
use of the resultant musical figure in the accompaniment as a
unifying expressive force. This was a concept to which Schubert
had already given expression in "Gretchen am Spinnrade" but the
importance of which no other composer seemed to seize upon. In
effect Schubert created a matrix to which the conflicting emotions
of the poem could be bound, a mood-setting presence which would
underly the entire poem whatever the vagaries of narrative
development.   As we shall see, Schubert chose a musical
equivalent for the droning of the spinning wheel as the
characteristic figure in "Gretchen am Spinnrade"; for "Erlkönig"
the sound of the furiously galloping steed was the obvious but
nonetheless brilliant choice.

Ex. I

Ex. II

The realization of Schubert's musical analogue for the hard-riding horse (Ex. I) is infamous among accompanists, many of whom—including some of the most renowned—have had to resort to simplification (breaking the octaves) when faced with the relentlessly pounding triplet octaves and chords with which the right hand is burdened for 57 bars at the beginning and 49 measures toward the end of the song. (Weight-lifting has been suggested, perhaps facetiously perhaps not, as the best preparation for the pianist.) Only in the Elfking's first two appeals to the lad do the right-hand triplets relent, but even in these verses the basic rhythm continues (Ex. II).

The oft-repeated upward scale-downward triad figure in the accompaniment's bass line (see Ex. I above), integral to the music's compelling rhythmic force and its overall sense of foreboding, is of course part of the basic musical analogue for the horse's frenzied gallop. Although there are exceptions, this figure is usually heard when the voice is silent, and never appears when the Elfking is singing his seductive verses.

The song begins with a fifteen-bar piano introduction. In addition to the tension-producing triplets and scale-figure already mentioned, this rather long prelude includes a chromatic rise in bars six and seven and a sudden drop in dynamic level in bar thirteen, both of which add to its dramatic force. Schubert shows great self-confidence in beginning with such ferocity, for he knows he will have to increase the pitch continually to keep the song moving to its climax.

The singer, first appearing in the role of the narrator, is able to enter quietly over the now softly rumbling accompaniment. (Although there is a stunning recording of it by Elizabeth Schwarzkopf and other women have performed it, the song is usually sung by a male.) The opening vocal phrase is a tight melisma on the note A, the subdominant, but for the second phrase it expands into a tonic triad. The question asked by these first two melodic phrases is answered dramatically ("Es ist der Vater mit seinem Kind") with a soaring melodic line and cadential moves from the tonic G minor to B flat, its relative major. Even as the words speak of the security with which the father holds his son in his arms, the ominous scale-figure in the bass of the accompaniment warns the listener to beware.

A brief piano interlude marks the poem's strophic division, after which the singer enters again, this time as the voice of the father. Here the chromatically-rising melody betrays the apprehension Schubert thinks the father must be feeling, despite the soothing nature of the words given him by Goethe. Switching roles once again, the singer now presents the boy's frightened query: "Siehst, Vater, du den Erlkönig nicht?" As Goethe called attention to the "du" by its placement in the sentence, Schubert emphasizes it by its down-beat placement in the measure and its high (E flat) pitch. At all times in this first appeal by the youth, the melodic notes are consonant with the accompanying harmonies. The father's answer, separated from the boy's question by five beats of the characteristic accompanying material, is terse and limited to small intervals. It is followed by a piano interlude briefer than the first, but still long enough to indicate the end of one strophe and the beginning of another.

At Strophe III we hear the voice of the Elfking himself. Schubert's rhythm (three beats each on "geh" and "mir") and the gently pulsating figure to which the accompaniment now changes soften the potential harshness of Goethe's "komm, geh mit mir," and the whole section is sweetly consonant. A sudden *forte* at the boy's "Mein Vater, mein Vater," introduced abruptly with no musical pause between stanzas, startles the listener. The lad's increasing anxiety is emphasized by the clash between the E flat of his melody and the D octaves in the accompaniment under most of the first part of his question and the chromatic rise which completes it.

This time the father's answer seems less controlled, less secure, as he assures his son that what he hears is only the wind rustling in the dry leaves. In contrast, the Elfking, who speaks next, remains calm and pleasant, his gracefully sinuous melody curving over simple, major harmonies played in a flowing triplet eighth-note pattern (Ex. III)

Once again the frenzied music of the boy's plaint breaks out without warning. This time Schubert leaves only a single measure break between Strophes V and VI, repeating the musical analogue of dissonance (the melody's F against the accompaniment's E) to express the boy's fears. Since the pitch is now higher than it was the first time we heard this clash at "Mein Vater, mein Vater," the emotion is intensified (Ex. IV); it will be made still more telling at the boy's final cry—where he says the Elfking has hurt him— when the clashing notes are even higher (G flat and F).

Ex. III

Ex. IV

As we have pointed out, during most of the song the rising scale pattern in the accompaniment is heard primarily during solo piano passages. At the final strophe, when the narrator has once again become the speaker, this ominous pattern is heard every other measure even though the vocal line is continuous. It is as though there is too little time left for the former polite alternation to prevail—everything in the music is racing towards the tragic denouement (the section is marked *accelerando*). And what a denouement! At the final word of the penultimate verse the music begins to fade, coming to a halt on a *pianissimo* A flat major chord. "In seinen Armen das Kind" is sung in an unaccompanied recitative, after which a diminished chord prepares the ear for the last two words, "war tot." It is left to the accompaniment to bring this incomplete cadence around to a full close with simple V-I chords.

There are surely songs more subtle, more endearing, more beautiful than "Erlkönig" in the vast Schubert catalogue, but it would be difficult, if not impossible, to find one more dramatic, more filled with emotion, more suited to its text than this ever-popular work.

GRETCHEN AM SPINNRADE   Goethe

"Gretchen am Spinnrade" is one of several "songs"—that is, poems the characters were actually supposed to sing—written by Goethe as part of his great drama *Faust*. Two other such pieces, Gretchen's touching little ballad about the ever-faithful King of Thule (a nice piece of dramatic irony when contrasted to the affair she will soon have with Faust) and Mephistopheles' satiric ditty about a King's favorite Flea (a barely masked and hence rather daring political statement), have been set by important composers, and, like "Gretchen am Spinnrade," are encountered as solo songs. Several others, such as Gretchen's prayer to the *Mater Dolorosa* and the song of the Rat (like "The Flea," part of the drinking scene at a beer-cellar in Leipzig), seem more wedded to their original purpose and are less well-known.

Goethe worked on his retelling of the ancient Faust legend all his life. The definitive version of Part I, considerably changed from its earlier "Urfaust" appearance in 1790, was published in 1808, but Goethe refused to authorize the release of Part II, which he constantly rewrote, until after his death in 1832.

Although he utilized several available sources for much of his plot, Goethe himself created the story of Faust's involvement with Gretchen, thereby changing the old tale irrevocably. In fact Gretchen's story, because it is the most moving part of Goethe's *Faust* as well as the sole subject of the opera Gounod based on it, has become for most people the most memorable aspect of the legend. This may very well have been the poet's intention, for he saw the history of mankind, though in itself non-tragic, unfolding "through countless objectively necessary individual tragedies" like that suffered by Gretchen.[5] Her story is the particular through

which the universal may be seen and studied. It shows the tragic
conflict between man and woman, between the demands made by
the species' inexorable striving for improvement, as exemplified by
Faust's continued quest for knowledge and experience, and the
contradictory needs of the individual—here Gretchen's desire for
a permanent tie to Faust. Furthermore, for Goethe love was not
only 'real,' it was a "quasi-religious phenomenon...the surrender
of oneself to a higher spiritual entity [which] could and did expand
to encompass the whole of a person's universe." Thus, "when it
went wrong the lover could say, with Gretchen...'the whole world
has turned to gall for me.'"[6]

GRETCHEN AM SPINNRADE

Meine Ruh ist hin,
Mein Herz ist schwer;
ich finde sie nimmer
Und nimmermehr.

Wo ich ihn nicht hab,
Ist mir das Grab,
Die ganze Welt
Ist mir vergällt.

Mein armer Kopf
Ist mir verrückt,
Mein armer Sinn
Ist mir zerstückt.

Meine Ruh ist hin,
Mein Herz ist schwer,
Ich finde sie nimmer
Und nimmermehr.

Nach ihm nur schau ich
Zum Fenster hinaus,
Nach ihm nur geh ich
Aus dem Haus.

Sein hoher Gang,
Sein' edle Gestalt,
Seines Mundes Lächeln,
Seiner Augen Gewalt,

Und seiner Rede
Zauberfluß,
Sein Händedruck,
Und ach, sein Kuß!

Meine Ruh ist hin,
Mein Herz ist schwer,
Ich finde sie nimmer
Und nimmermehr.

Mein Busen drängt
Sich nach ihm hin.
Ach, dürft ich fassen
Und halten ihn!

Und küssen ihn,
So wie ich wollt,
An seinen Küssen
Vergehen sollt.

GRETCHEN AT THE SPINNING WHEEL

My peace is gone,
My heart is heavy;
I'll never find it
And nevermore.

Where I do not have him
There is my grave,
The whole world
Is gall to me.

My poor head
Is crazy,

My poor mind
Is torn apart.

My peace is gone,
My heart is heavy,
Never do I find it
And nevermore.

For him only I look
Out my window,
For him only I go
Out of the house.

His lofty motion,
His noble form,
The smile of his mouth,
The force of his eyes

And the flow of his speech
Like magic,
The press of his hand,
And, oh, his kiss!

My peace is gone.
My heart is heavy,
I find it never
And nevermore.

My bosom swells
Only for him,
Oh, that I might hold him
And clasp him

And kiss him,
As much as I want,
I should lose myself
In his kisses!

By the time we see Gretchen at her spinning wheel, she has already been seduced and abandoned by Faust. Despite the fact that her beloved brother and mother have both perished as a result of her passion for her fickle lover, she feels no remorse, only the ache of his absence, the need for his embrace. Her thoughts are as obsessive as the mindless motion of her wheel, returning to the same phrases over and over. Strophe I is repeated as Strophe IV and then again as Strophe VIII, and there is repetition within single strophes: the opening "Mein Ruh ist hin" and "Mein Herz ist schwer" as well as "nimmer" and "nimmermehr"; "Mein armer Kopf" and "Mein armer Sinn" in Strophe III; "Nach ihm nur schau ich" and "Nach ihm nur geh ich" in Strophe V; all four verses of Strophe VI beginning with some form of "Sein," and so forth.

By giving two stressed syllables in each of the poem's brief verses, Goethe creates an obsessive rhythm to match the girl's repetitive thoughts and the equally repetitive gestures necessary to her task. The confused syntax of the last two lines may reflect the rush of emotion which floods through Gretchen at the thought of kissing Faust to her heart's content, just as the wildly irregular rhyme scheme used throughout the poem may be a poetic analogue for her lack of control. The picture of the heroine spinning at a wheel and the use of the archaic "nimmer" instead of "nie" for "never" remind us that the time of this scene is in the far-off past, but the power of its emotions convince us that Gretchen's feelings might have been shared by many a young woman in Goethe's own time.

Ex. I

Schubert begins his setting of "Gretchen am Spinnrade" with a brief piano prelude which establishes the minor tonality of the piece while providing the perfect musical analogue for the

monotonous humming of the spinningwheel (Ex. I). The piano's
figure expresses both the whirring of the wheel (right hand) and
the rhythmic impetus necessary to keep it spinning (left hand).

The pattern is, of course, a stroke of genius, allowing as it does
for all sorts of subtle Schubertian modulations. The most telling
of these occurs when Gretchen's absorption in her own pain yields
to her vivid memories of Faust. The music expresses this change
in her thoughts by moving from minor to major (Ex. II).

Ex. II

Schubert changes Goethe's poem in one minor and one major
way: in the third line of the oft-repeated first strophe, he reiterates
"ich finde," extending that verse to nine syllables and giving it
three beats instead of the original two. More important for the
meaning of the text, he ends the song with yet one more statement
of the initial strophe. This alteration is significant because, while
Goethe leaves Gretchen in the midst of her ecstatic reverie,
Schubert brings her back to her self-aborption, her pain, her
despair. Instead of a single upward direction, we thus have a
cyclical one, allowing the song to end as it began on the original
piano figure in the original key.

While the climax of the poem may be seen as its last verse, the
climactic moment of the song is undoubtedly where Gretchen feels
once again, albeit only in her fantasy, her lover's passionate
embrace. At the "ach" just preceding "sein Kuß," the piano figure
is halted abruptly by a *sforzando* chord; the voice is silent, while
the piano has a second accented chord; and then comes the V-I rise
to the highest note in the piece (G in the D minor high-voice
version). The *fermata* in both parts at this point emphasizes the
break in the continuity of the music, an analogue for a break in the
spinning yarn. It is clear that the tension aroused in Gretchen by

her erotic day-dream has made her spin too fast; to make this all
the more obvious Schubert marks the music preceding the break
crescendo and *accelerando* (Ex. III)

Ex. III

For a while Gretchen cannot get the spinning wheel started
again, but on the third attempt, once again brilliantly evoked by
Schubert's music, the whirring motion resumes (Ex. IV).

Evidently preoccupation with the mechanics of her task—an idea
not expressed in the original poem—has brought Gretchen out of
her reverie, for the words she sings after the spinningwheel starts

up again, an event we again infer only from the music, are the by now familiar "Meine Ruh ist hin, mein Herz ist schwer." Never again in the song—and this is actually contrary to the feeling of the poem—is Gretchen able to forget her pain and longing.

Ex.IV

It would be hard to deny the effectiveness of "Gretchen am Spinnrade" either as Goethe's poem or as Schubert's song, but at least for this reader-listener, the psychological message conveyed by the seventeen-year old Schubert has more validity: Gretchen will be able to deny her real situation only—as Goethe himself recognizes—in Ophelia-like madness. Her obsessive repetition of thoughts and words in the song is a step towards that madness.

GANYMED   Goethe

> Wie im Morgenglanze
> Du rings mich anglühst,
> Frühling, Geliebter!
> Mit tausendfacher Liebeswonne

Sich an mein Herze drängt
Deiner ewigen Wärme
Heilig Gefühl
Unendlich Schöne!

Daß ich dich fassen möcht
In diesen Arm!

Ach, an deinem Busen
Lieg ich schmachte,
Und deine Blumen, dein Gras
Drängen sich an mein Herz.
Du kühlst den brennenden
Durst meines Busens,
Lieblicher Morgenwind,
Ruft drein die Nachtigall
Liebend nach mir aus dem Nebeltal.

Ich komm, ich komme!
Wohin? Ach, wohin?

Hinauf! hinauf strebt's,
Es schweben die Wolken
Abwärts, die Wolken
Neigen sich der sehnenden Liebe.
Mir! mir!
In eurem Schoße
Aufwärts!
Umfangend umfangen!
Aufwärts an deinen Busen,
Alliebender Vater!

GANYMEDE

How your glow envelops me
In the morning radiance,
Spring, my beloved!
With love's thousandfold joy
The hallowed sensation

Of your eternal warmth
Floods my heart,
Infinite beauty!

O that I might clasp you
In these arms!

Ah, on your breast
I lie languishing,
And your flowers, your grass
Press close to my heart.
You cool the burning
Thirst in my breast,
Sweet morning breeze,
As the nightingale calls
Tenderly to me from the misty valley.

I come, I come!
But where? Ah where?

Upwards! strive upwards!
The clouds drift
Down, yielding
To yearning love,
To me, to me!
In your lap,
Upwards,
Embracing and embraced!
Upwards to your bosom,
All-loving Father!

Goethe's "Ganymed" is an expression of the longing for an
ecstatic union with nature often found in German poetry of this
pre-Romantic, *Sturm und Drang* period (the poem was written in
1774). Bordering on the erotic, this type of poetry has little in
common with the French Romantics' feeling about nature. Even
in Rousseau's famous description of a storm on Lake Geneva or
Lamartine's seminal "Le Lac," for example, the protagonist is

central and nature's function is to reflect, contradict or ignore his moods or experiences.

In "Ganymed" on the other hand, Goethe longs to be at one with the all-encompassing cosmos. He expresses a "rapturous acceptance of his personal destiny,"[7] a willingness to submerge his identity, his personal story, in the pantheistic radiance he feels emanating from above. The closest one comes in the song literature to this kind of obliteration of the self in an infinite cosmic embrace is in the Belgian Symbolist Charles van Lerberghe's cycle *Chanson d'Eve* as set to music by Gabriel Fauré. Beginning with "le premier matin du monde" and ending with the desire for absorption in "la mort, poussière d'étoiles," this cycle marvels at "Comme Dieu rayonne" with much the same erotic fervor conveyed by Goethe.

And erotic it is! The word "Liebe" (loved one) appears in one form or another six times in the piece ("Geliebter," "Liebeswonne," "Lieblicher," "Liebend," "Liebe" and "Alliebender"). From "Frühling, Geliebter / Mit tausendfacher Liebeswonne" in the first strophe, to the unrhymed couplet "Dass ich dich fassen möcht / In diesen Arm"; from "Ach, an deinem Busen / Lieg ich, schmachte" to "Du kühlst den brennenden / Durst meines Busens" of Strophe II; and concluding with the final stanza's "die Wolken / Neigen sich der sehnenden Liebe" and "Umfangend, umfangen!", the vocabulary is that of physical passion. The message, however, concerns a different sort of ecstasy than that granted to most humans. It is a quasi-mystical emotion in which gender is overlooked. The poet wants to sit in the lap of and be embraced on the bosom of the All-loving Father, although "lap" and "bosom" are more often symbols of maternity; and he speaks of a "beloved" (Geliebter) but masculine "Spring" (Frühling) which he wants to "clasp in these arms."

Appropriate to the passion it describes is the freedom of form and elliptical style of "Ganymed." There are few rhymed end-sounds, and those that do exist (Nachtigall / Nebeltal in the central strophe, for example) seem incidental if not actually accidental. Verses are of uneven length whether measured by syllable-count or metric accent, and the stanzas are separated into eight, two, nine, two, and ten-line units respectively. The syntax is difficult, perhaps intentionally ambiguous at times, and there is

even some temporal confusion, for the nightingale is said to call to
the poet in the sweet morning breeze.   While clouds drift down,
the poet's ultimate movement is upward, from his passive languishing on Spring's radiant breast to his active striving for the cosmic
embrace of the All-loving Father.   At no time are we told who
Ganymed is.   (In Greek mythology he is Hebe's successor as
cup-bearer for the Gods; a beautiful Trojan youth, originally
mortal, he was abducted by Zeus because of his beauty and flown
to Olympus on the back of an eagle.) Those who know the legend
may see in the poem a personalized and impassioned retelling of
it.

From the placid triadic statement with which the song's piano
prelude begins and the composer's *Etwas langsam* (somewhat
deliberate) instruction to the performers, it is clear that Schubert
sees the mood of the opening of "Ganymed" as tranquil and
serene.   The voice's opening phrases also move at this gentle,
pleasant pace, with long notes on the strong syllables obviating any
feeling of urgency.   Although there is a bit more motion in the
vocal line for "Frühling, Geliebter," the rhythmic extension of two
of the five syllables in that line of text (each is set to a rather
broad two-note interval) and the presence of a full cadence at the
end of the line prevent any real sense of acceleration.

A shift from quarter-notes to eighth-notes for the basic rhythmic
pulse in both accompaniment and melody begins to move things
along at "Mit tausendfacher Liebeswonne." The lovely change
from major to minor at "ewigen Wärme," a typical Schubertian
moment full of poignant yearning, seems dictated by a purely
musical impulse, as there is nothing in the poem at this point to
suggest it.   Schubert brings the first strophe to a close with a
dramatic climax triggered by a measure-long chord on the second
syllable of "unendliche" (unending, infinite) (Ex. I).

Ex. I

The ensuing couplet is set to a somewhat trivial, albeit
charming, figure, and no musical division marks its conclusion or
the beginning of the next full-length stanza. To suit his metric
plan or perhaps to make the sentence easier to follow, Schubert
changes the second line of Strophe III a bit, replacing the original
"Lieg ich, schmachte" with "Lieg ich und schmachte," ("I lie and
languish" instead of "I lie, languish"). Goethe's choice is more
elliptical and hence more intense, but it would be hard to make the
essential comma audible without a considerable pause between
"ich" and "schmachte," a device Schubert obviously did not care
to use at this point (Ex. II).

Ex. II

A piano interlude between the fourth and fifth lines of the
central strophe give a false impression of the way the poem is
actually divided, a liberty Schubert had not taken with the two
Goethe texts previously discussed. An onomatopoeic trill sets
"Morgenwind" and is then repeated to form another brief interlude.

It is not until the introduction to the ecstatic words "Ich komm!
ich komme!" that Schubert's music, lovely as it has been per se,
finally captures the rapturous urgency of Goethe's poem. Now all
at once the composer seems to find perfect musical analogues for
the poet's thoughts: the discords under both instances of "wohin?",
created by *appoggiaturas*, to express the short-lived anxiety of the
protagonist (Ex. III), the mounting exaltation of the rising line
given to the repeated "Hinauf strebt's, hinauf!" (again a small
alteration in the text by Schubert) (Ex. IV), the growing excitement
created by the accompaniment's new rhythmic figure for "Mir!

mir!" and the words that follow (Ex. V)—these all enhance and enrich the poem.

Ex. III

Ex. IV

Ex. V

Schubert's musical portrayal of "Alliebender Vater!" is more problematic, for it breaks the onrush of emotion by setting the "All-loving Father" apart from the preceding material. One senses that Schubert's is a Christian "Father," a gentle, sublime, but somewhat remote figure, not a pagan like Zeus who can and does rush down from the sky to scoop up a youth for his own purposes just because the lad is so lovely to look at. Nevertheless, the leitmotiv given "Alliebender Vater" is elegant (Ex. VI), and Schubert makes effective use of it.

Ex. VI

With this first presentation of "Alliebender Vater" Schubert has brought the music to an incomplete cadence on the dominant of the F major tonality which he established at the beginning of the final stanza and on which he intends to close the song (analyzed in the key for high voice). To extend the piece he repeats the last strophe from the words "die Wolken" (middle of the second line) to the conclusion of the poem, and—with some intensification—he reiterates the musical ideas he had already affixed to this part of the text. As a final coda he repeats "Alliebender Vater" yet again, and then allows the piano to close the song with a series of rising chords, most of them on the tonic, but with a lovely suspension at the very end. Each time "Alliebender Vater" is sung, its melody becomes longer and more elaborate (three measures at first hearing, four-and-a-half bars for the second, six for the last), so these two words come to dominate the song. Here one can only guess at Goethe's possible reaction to this emphasis.

For some critics Schubert's setting vitiates the power of Goethe's "Ganymed," neutralizing its force as it slows "the pace with which the sounds, ideas and images succeed one another" in the original text.[8] But a case might be made for the way in which Schubert saves the exhilaration and exaltation which is clearly in the poem for the final stanza. By at first emphasizing the languor which is also in the text, he makes the rapturous "Ich komm, ich komme!" and the upward soaring that follows all the more telling because of the music's tranquil beginning. In any case, the song is beautiful, and retains a well-deserved place in the repertoire.

DER TOD UND DAS MÄDCHEN   Claudius

Matthias Claudius (1740-1815), a Northern German by birth, was an all-around man of letters whose poetry and prose are noted for their directness, simplicity and harmony. One senses a strong affinity for the folklore and folk-poetry of the German people in Claudius' work—a genuine naiveté which, at least in "Death and the Maiden," is tremendously effective.

DER TOD UND DAS MÄDCHEN

Das Mädchen: Vorüber! ach, vorüber!
          Geh, wilder Knochenmann!
          Ich bin noch jung, geh, Lieber!
          Und rühre mich nicht an.

Der Tod: Gib deine Hand, du schön und zart Gebild!
          Bin Freund und komme nicht zu strafen.
          Sei gutes Muts! ich bin nicht wild,
          Sollst sanft in meinen Armen schlafen!

DEATH AND THE MAIDEN

The Maiden: Pass on, oh, pass on!
              Go, cruel man of death [literally boneman]!
              I am still young, go, please!
              And do not touch me.

Death: Give me your hand, you lovely and tender
                creature!
              I am a friend and do not come to punish.
              Be of good courage! I am not cruel,
              You shall sleep softly in my arms!

Like so many folk-poems, "Death and the Maiden," which was written in 1774, is a dialogue. The young girl speaks first, in short, breathless, off-balance phrases that mirror her fear and confusion.   Urgently she repeats her plea—"Vorüber, ach, vorüber! / geh,...geh, Lieber!" Only in her last sentence is the pace made slower, perhaps to portray exhaustion, perhaps to signal the beginning of resignation or the possibility of acceptance.

The second strophe, Death's response, is linked to the first by their shared ABAB rhyme scheme, but is remarkably different in tone and tempo. While the Maiden's speeches are flustered and repetitious, Death speaks in measured, weighty cadences. Of the ten syllables in his first sentence, six would normally receive strong accents, necessitating a fairly slow reading. The first natural emphasis in his second statement, "Bin Freund und komme nicht zu strafen," falls on "Freund" (friend), starting the phrase off with a reassuring quality.   "Sei gutes Muts!", with its archaic use of "gutes" for good, has a biblical and hence authoritative ring, adding to Death's verisimilitude. The open a sounds in "sanft," "Armen" and "schlafen", the softly sibilant s's in "sollst" and "sanft," and the caressing *schl* of "schlafen" reinforce the appealing gentleness of the message of the last line: "You shall sleep softly in my arms."

And yet one senses ambivalence in this apparently naive poem. Why, for example, is "Lieber" capitalized, making it appear to be a noun? Could the maiden be thinking of Death as a seductive

lover? Is she as attracted as she is repelled by the advances of this
"man of bones"? Certainly the choice of "ruhre" (move, stir,
touch) as the verb in her last sentence can be seen as having erotic
connotations. As for Death, his words can be taken at their face
value as genuinely kind and gentle, or interpreted as those of a
wily, evil seducer (should one emphasize "nicht" or "strafen" in
'Bin Freund und komme nicht zu strafen," for example?). Death
as religious solace, as the ultimate consolation, and Death as evil
seducer are both common folk motifs.

Schubert's setting of "Death and the Maiden" was composed in
1817. Seven years later he used its principal theme for the
variation movement of his D Minor Quartet #14, which is therefore called "The Death and the Maiden Quartet".

The song begins with great solemnity. Its theme is introduced
in the minor mode as a piano prelude, abandoned during the
Maiden's stanza, referred to in the accompaniment (still in the
minor) when Death answers the maiden, and ultimately transformed to the major mode for the piano postlude with which the
piece ends (the key for high voice is hence listed as D
minor-major). This marvelous music is heard only in the piano
part. Played in the piano's lower register, in its minor
manifestation it is solemn, stately and somewhat funereal, although
according to the composer's instructions it is to be paced at a
moderate ("Maßig") rather than at a lugubrious tempo (Ex. I).

Ex. I

The principal theme is separated from the singer's entrance by a
brief pause. The tempo then picks up for the Maiden's agitated
words ("Etwas geschwinder," rather quickly, says the composer)

which are sung in short, disconnected phrases and are underscored
by *non-legato* chords (Ex. II).

Ex. II

Ex. III

Tension mounts as the singer's melodic line rises in pitch. A
pleading quality is introduced by the falling interval at "bin noch
jung" and intensified by a still wider falling interval on "Lieber."
Up to the word "Lieber" the music has been primarily in minor or
diminished harmonies; at that significant word Schubert gives us
a C seven chord which leads to F major (the relative major to D
minor). He then completes the Maiden's stanza in the major mode
and with new-found tranquility, repeating her last verse ("und
rühre mich nicht an") to allow enough time for the change in the

music to be effective.

A brief piano interlude, played very quietly and followed by a long silence, precedes Death's response. Death's first sixteen syllables are solemnly declaimed on one note—the tonic—while the accompaniment plays chords derived from the opening statement in the original minor mode. A subtle dissonance, related to the third chord of the principal theme but made a little more obvious here by the rising bass line, follows the word "Freund" (Ex.III).

At "zu strafen" C seven chords once again prepare for the same change to the relative major that introduced the Maiden's last verse. Again the singer's line is declamatory, with eight syllables on the new (temporary) tonic (F) followed by seven syllables on D. A full cadence brings us to D major on the singer's last syllable, after which the piano plays the original theme in the peaceful, consoling major modality.

In his setting Schubert has chosen to see Death as an unambiguously comforting figure—if there is a hint of menace in the faint discord after "Freund," it is completely dissipated by the conclusion of the song. We are convinced by the tranquil, major ending Schubert writes for her stanza that the girl's agitation, made all the more palpable by the music of her first three verses, is soothed even before Death begins to speak, and, obviously, there is a quasi-religious consolation in the major-mode postlude.

Could Schubert have introduced more ambiguity into the song? Could he have added to its interest by giving it a multi-dimensional reading? Perhaps, but who among us would really wish it other than it is?

STÄNDCHEN   Rellstab

Leise flehen meine Lieder
Durch die Nacht zu dir;
In den stillen Hain hernieder,
Liebchen, komm zu mir!

Flüsternd schlanke Wipfel rauschen
In des Mondes Licht,
Des Verräters feindlich Lauschen
fürchte, Holde, nicht.

Hörst die Nachtigallen schlagen?
Ach! sie flehen dich,
Mit der Töne süßen Klagen
Flehen sie für mich.

Sie verstehn des Busens Sehnen,
Kennen Liebesschmerz,
Ruhren mit den Silbertönen
Jēdes weiche Herz.

Laß auch dir die Brust bewegen,
Liebchen, höre mich!
Bebend harr ich dir entgegen
Komm, beglücke mich!

SERENADE

My songs softly plead to you
Through the night;
Into the quiet meadow down here,
Loved one, come to me!

Whispering slender treetops
Rustle in the moonlight,
Dear one, do not fear
The hostile spying of those who would betray.

Do you hear the nightingales singing?
Oh! they beg you
With the sweet plaintive sound
They plead for me.

They understand the bosom's longing,
They know the pain of love,
They touch with silvery tones
Each soft heart.

Let your breast also be moved,
Darling, hear me!
Trembling I wait for you!
Come, make me happy!

This appealing poem by a minor figure named Ludwig Rellstab (1799-1860) is a compendium of the tropes of the times: nightingales, used as the symbol of lyric poetry since that metaphor was first expressed by thirteenth-century writer Gottfried von Strassburg; the gentle melancholy of as yet unconsummated love (according to the German medieval tradition, *Der Nachtigallenchor* or chorus of nightingales—the extended metaphor for lyric poetry as a whole—*stopped* singing when love was fulfilled);[9] the "whispering treetops" as a synecdoche for the forest in which lovers traditionally seek refuge and consolation; the moonlight by which such scenes are always dimly illuminated; the secret words which no eavesdropper will overhear—these are the figures in which the pre-Sturm-und-Drang "Sentimentalists"[10] revelled.

Friedrich Gottlieb Klopstock (1724-1803) is the best known of these poets; what distinguished them from the full-blown Romantics who followed, is a certain all-purpose melancholy, a lack of specific, individual pain or passion, a passivity of sentiment whose main purpose seems to be the "cultivation and enjoyment of an indistinct mood."[11] Although Rellstab's dates place him with the later group, and despite his references to the "longing [and] pain of love," "Ständchen" reverberates with the earlier, gentler, sweeter sentiments expressed by Klopstock and his immediate disciples. This in no way detracts from its charm.

Technically, "Ständchen" is adroit without being remarkable. Its ABAB rhyme scheme is typical of the lyric, as is its alternation of feminine and masculine end-sounds. Its regular trochaic (strong, weak) meter, interrupted as it is by the single-syllable stressed endings of all the even-numbered lines (the sole excep-

tion is "Liebesschmerz" which ends the second line of the fourth
strophe, but since "Schmerz" is in itself a common word, the use
of this compound does not really alter the effect), provides a
soothing lilt while avoiding monotony. The whispery sounds of
the second strophe are delightfully onomatopoeic, and the whole
poem abounds in "süßen Tone," none the less effective for being
somewhat conventional.

Since every "Ständchen," and the number is legion, calls to
mind a young man plaintively singing to the accompaniment of his
lute or guitar under the balcony or window of his beloved,
Schubert's "plucked-chord" introduction to this particular "Ständchen" is more or less to be expected. So too is the gently
melancholic minor mode (D for high voice) of this opening—we
must believe that the lover is suffering a little while he pleads his
case Ex. I)

Ex. I

The simple chords continue as the singer enters. Long notes on
"flehen" and "Lieder" alter the rhythm of the text by making of
the preceding "Leise" and "meine" relatively weak, unaccented feet
(their inner assonances are, however, still apparent). At the end
of each couplet the piano echoes the singer's last phrase, providing
a sweetly yearning, evenly flowing melody (the cross-rhythm of
the upper-voice's triplet against the bass's regular eighth-notes at
the ends of these phrases is a subtle touch of sophistication in this
otherwise extremely simple material). The music for the second
half of the strophe is an intensification of that of the first, with
wider intervals and higher pitches in the vocal line.

At the end of the first strophe, Schubert moves from the minor
to the major—his preferred modal direction. Instead of a piano
interlude after the next couplet, we have a duet, with the singer
repeating the second line of melody and text while the piano plays

the same melody a third higher. Since the piano is on top, the voice seems to accompany it instead of the other way around (Ex. II).

Ex. II

Ex. III

Except for the ending, which Schubert alters to prepare for the new material which is to come, the music for the two couplets of Strophe II is the same.

An eight-bar piano interlude—or perhaps one should say a twice-heard four-bar passage—separates Strophes I and II from Stanzas III and IV, to which Schubert gives a setting identical to that of the beginning. Matching the modest tone of urgency which distinguishes the last strophe from the preceding four, Schubert begins this last segment with a rising pattern (a sequentially stated

A major chord) in which dotted eighths and sixteenth-notes figure. Instead of waiting for the voice to conclude and then echoing it or joining it in a duet, the piano's statement of this new melodic line overlaps that of the singer, adding to the sense of urgency (Ex. III).

For the last pleading line, "Komm, beglücke mich!", Schubert brings back the ending he had used for each of the previous strophes. The first time we hear those words, the singer is accompanied by the characteristic guitar-like chords; the second time we have the by-now familiar duet as well as the chords, and the third time—yes, Schubert gives the serenader yet another repeat—they are sung to the long, sighing notes of a descending melodic line. The piano ends the song with a repeat of the material in its interlude between Strophes II and III, adding two reassuring bars in optimistic D major for the tranquil conclusion.

Of Schubert's last fourteen songs, published posthumously as *Schwanengesang (Swan song)*, seven, including "Ständchen," are settings of poems by Rellstab. (The other six are "Liebesbotschaft," "Kriegers Ahnung," "Frühlingsbotschaft," "Aufenthalt," "In der Ferne," and "Abschied.") By far the most popular of the group, "Ständchen" is hauntingly lovely in its sweet simplicity. Like its text, it avoids the Scylla and Charybdis of maudlin sentimentality and cold impersonality, expressing time-honored feelings through time-honored conventions. It is quite possible that Schubert's music raises the poem that inspired it above its intrinsic merits, but—difficult as it is to disassociate the two in a piece as familiar as this—one can only accept the composer's treatment with gratitude.

DER DOPPELGÄNGER   Heine

Heinrich Heine (1797-1856) is somewhat of an anomaly among German poets of his age. The first person of acknowledged Jewish descent to achieve fame as a German-language man of letters, expatriated for the last eight years of his life (completely paralyzed by some dreadful disease, he lived in Paris, bedridden, supported by a pension from the French government, from 1848 until his death), Heine was at once the most cosmopolitan of writers and the "master of *Volkslied*" who "gave immortal form" to the intensely national legend of *Die Lorelei*.[12] (The equally famous "Die beiden Grenadiere," set so effectively by Robert Schumann, is also his, and the Nazis had a devil of a time "expurgating" these two poems and the many songs composed for them from their Aryan musico-literary canon.)

Published in 1827, Heine's Buch der Lieder, from which "Der Doppelgänger" is taken, made its author the most popular poet in Germany (Goethe was at this time considered somewhat old-fashioned and was hence in temporary eclipse). It also established Heine's international reputation.

The poems in *Buch der Lieder*, many of which begin with the personal pronoun "ich," were assumed to be autobiographical when they first appeared, apparently having as their source their creator's unhappy love affair with a young woman named Amalie. More contemporary appraisals see the author of these love poems as "transcending subjectivity by constructing poetic fictions."[13] Since Heine was a master of irony, which deepened to bitter satire as he grew older, and since many of his most personal poems employ the mood-breaking device known as *Stimmungsbrechung* (negating or ridiculing in the final line of text the aura created by the bulk of the poem), this latter-day assessment seems plausible. But it is also possible that Heine's notorious pleasure in blowing brilliantly opalescent (but soapy) bubbles and then deliberately pricking them,"[14] may have been a result of embarrassment at his own sincere sentiments, or—even worse—at the triteness of these emotions.[15] Neither case is subject to proof, and—since "Der Doppelgänger" is not one of the poems ending with a *Stimmungs-brechung*—we need not belabor the issue.

DER DOPPELGÄNGER

Still ist die Nacht, es ruhen die Gassen,
In diesem Hause wohnte mein Schatz;
Sie hat schon längst die Stadt verlassen,
Doch steht noch das Haus auf demselben Platz.

Da steht auch ein Mensch und starrt in die Höhe,
Und ringt die Hände vor Schmerzensgewalt;
Mir graust es, wenn ich sein Antlitz sehe
Der Mond zeigt mir meine eigne Gestalt

Du Doppelgänger, du bleicher Geselle!
Was äffst du nach mein Liebesleid,
Das mich gequält auf dieser Stelle
So manche Nacht, in alter Zeit?

THE DOUBLE

Still is the night, tranquil the allée,
In this house where my love lived;
She left the city so long ago,
But the house still stands in the same place.

There also stands a man, and he stares upward,
And wrings his hands because of the strength of his pain;
I am horrified, when I see his countenance
The moon shows me my own shape.

You doppelgänger, you pale companion!
Why do you mimic my love-caused pain,
Which tortured me on this spot
So many nights, in time long past?

"Der Doppelgänger" begins with a simple yet evocative statement: "Still is the night." The lane ("street" seems too prosaic a
translation for Gassen, perhaps the French allée comes closer) is
also tranquil, continues the first line of verse, and the second line
informs us matter-of-factly that the narrator's "darling lived in this
house." The last two lines of the first stanza tell the read-
er/listener that she, his "Schatz," left the city long ago, and yet the
house still stands in the same place. The "doch" and "noch" of the
fourth line indicate that the narrator finds it paradoxical that the
external surroundings can remain unchanged after all that has
happened.

Strophe II brings a stranger onto the scene, a man who stands staring upward, wringing his hands because of the power of his pain ("Schmerzensgewalt"). We do not learn until the last three words of the stanza—"meine eigne Gestalt"—that the intruder and the narrator, who expresses his own horror at the revelation, are one and the same. In the final strophe the narrator addresses his double, his "Doppelgänger," with a bitter reproach: "Why do you mimic my love-pain?" he asks, "the pain that tortured me so many nights in olden times."

How are we to interpret this conclusion? Is the image the narrator has of himself a mockery of his true feelings? Is this one of those *Stimmungsbrechung* endings after all? Somehow, despite all one knows of Heine's bubble-breaking propensities, one cannot deny that the feeling of pain, of sorrow, even of horror expressed by the protagonist as he looks at his lost love, lost illusions, lost youth, is real.

The technique of the poem is conventional, with an ABAB rhyme scheme, four strong beats and a variable number of weak beats in each line, accented initial syllables at the beginning of each strophe and unaccented opening syllables thereafter. The first line is as balanced as a typical Victor Hugo sentence, and many other lines break naturally more or less midway. All but two—the third lines of the second and final strophes—have end punctuation, and even these verses do not lead to obvious *enjambements*.

Schubert's setting of "Der Doppelgänger," one of the six *Schwanengesang* with texts by Heine, was composed in the late summer or early autumn of 1828, that is, a few months before the composer's death. Unlike Goethe, who was a half-century older than Schubert and world-famous before the composer was born, Heine was probably unknown to the composer until January of 1828, when he heard some of the young poet's lyrics read at a meeting of the literary group to which he belonged. The speed with which he absorbed this material and then expressed its essence in music is, of course, typical of Schubert.

"Der Doppelgänger" begins with a sequence of four measure-long chords, played in the piano's lower registers. The absence of the interval of the third (the center of the triad and the note by which we distinguish major from minor) from two of these four chords gives them a hollow, preternatural sound, which is

augmented by the presence in all of them of the repeated F# (analyzed in B minor-major, the key for high voice). These chords
form a lugubrious, slow-moving melody which may be considered
the characteristic theme of the piece, although it is never taken up
by the vocal part (Ex. I).

Ex. I

When the voice enters, over a repeat of the four introductory
chords, it states the first phrase, "Still ist die Nacht," on one pitch,
the dominant F#. For "es ruhen die" the singer has a descending
tonic triad, but the phrase ends with yet another repeat of the F#
(Ex. II). In this first declamatory statement, Schubert honors
Heine's rhythmic pattern completely, providing one note for each
syllable and giving "Still" a quarter-note to assure its strength.

Ex. II

The second line of text is set more melismatically, with
ornamental extensions in the vocal part for "diesem," "Hause" and
"Schatz." The accompaniment's echo of the end of the vocal line,
which pulls the piano into the treble clef for the first time in the
song, is peculiarly plaintive. The next ten bars are a repeat of the
material just heard except for interesting alterations in the
melismas: "doch steht noch das Haus," the musical equivalent of

"in diesem Hause," is unadorned and syllabic, but there is an ornamental turn over "demselben."

As the second strophe begins, the piano's introductory chords once again provide background for the vocal part, but this time the *crescendo* marked by the composer and the rising line he gives to the singer make for a tremendous increase in tension, which finally explodes on a *fortissimo* D major chord and a climactic high F# at "vor Schmerzensgewalt." An octave drop and *decrescendo* at the last two syllables of that compound word place the strongest possible accent on the element in it that means "pain." (Ex. III)

Ex. III

Obsessively the characteristic chords begin again, bringing with them a second tension-producing *crescendo* and rising melodic line, this one similar to the first save for its culmination on the still higher pitch of G, which is left to reverberate through two measures. Now yet another B minor chord, played softly like the others and providing dramatic contrast to the tremendous triple *forte* of the climax just passed, introduces the chilling words "du Doppelgänger," all five syllables of which are intoned on the low F#. The eighth-note on "du" makes of it an unaccented upbeat, which may or may not have been Heine's intention. Schubert's use of the Devil's own interval (the "Diabolus in Musica," the tritone forbidden by medieval musicologists) arrests the listener's attention at the chord with which the second half of "Doppelgänger" is accompanied, for it is a strange and ominous variant to what has heretofore followed the tonic triad.

Strong chords and a third rise in the melodic line bring an angry final climax to the song at the words "so manche Nacht," but a sudden *piano* at "alter Zeit," which is sung with a gently curving melodic arch, seem to suggest the peace—or at least resignation—that time almost always brings to the sufferer of the pangs of unrequited love. To reaffirm the abatement of anguish with which Schubert wishes to leave us (would Heine have admitted this in his own experience?), the four characteristic chords are used twice as a postlude, the first time beginning as usual in the minor, the second time altered to accommodate a final major chord. Once again we have Schubert's favorite modal direction, from the minor to the major, but the change comes so late in the piece that the overall message of obsessive, almost hallucinatory pain, prevails.

Notes to Chapter II

1. J. C. Robertson, *A History of German Literature, Fifth Ed.* (British Book Center, 1966) p. 297.
2. Menhennet, pp. 120-123.
3. E. L. Stahl and W. E. Yuill, *German Literature in the 18th and 19th Centuries* (Barnes and Noble, 1970) p. 77.
4. From a lecture at New York's 92nd Street "Y" by Dr. Zeman during the 1990 Schubertiade (January 13, 1990)
5. Georg Lukacs, *Goethe and his Age* (Merlin Press, 1968, reprinted 1979, translation by Robert Anchor) pp. 179-180
6. Menhennet, p. 143.
7. Stahl and Yuill, p. 77.
8. Jack M. Stein, *Poem and Music in the German Lied.* Harvard University Press, 1971, p. 13.
9. Brody and Fowkes, p. 108.
10. Menhennet, p. 102.
11. Menhennet, p. 104.
12. Robertson, p. 426.
13. Stahl and Yuill, p. 220.
14. *The Penguin Book of German Verse with Introduction by Leonard Foster* (Penguin Books. 1959 Edition) p. xix.
15. Brody and Fowkes, p.95.

CHAPTER III

ROBERT SCHUMANN

FRAUENLIEBE UND -LEBEN
Adelbert von Chamisso

The *Frauenliebe und -leben* poems by Adelbert von Chamisso (1781-1838) have the dubious distinction of being the most adversely criticized in the entire art song repertoire. The reasons for this general disdain fall into two categories: the caliber of the poetry qua poetry, and the degree of verisimilitude of the psychological portrait it presents.

While modern critics are fairly unanimous in their negative appraisal of Chamisso's poetry, such was not always the general opinion. This scion of an aristocratic French family which was forced to flee its native land during the Reign of Terror was at one time admired for the "wonderful freshness of his lyrics" and the "warmth and sentimental naiveté [of his] wholly German" oeuvre.[1] That this latter quality should be especially noteworthy stems from the fact that the poet, equally at home in French and German and torn between them as a literary tongue, eschewed all "hint" of French aristocratic mannerismsms in his lyrics,[2] and this despite his friendship with such lions of the French literary world as Madame de Staël. (It was Madame de Staël who, with the knowledge of German literature she gleaned while exiled from France by Napoléon I, brought Goethe and other German writers to the attention of her own countrymen. Her *De l'Allemagne* of 1810 was particularly influential. Chamisso was her guest at Coppet, her residence-in-exile on Lake Geneva, for several months.)

An attempt on the part of this reader to divorce the sound of the poems in *Frauenliebe und -leben* from their sense has led to the mild conclusion that they are never less than skillful, and, that, with their easy, graceful flow and natural, unforced rhymes and rhythms, they sometimes rise above mere professionalism. That they could be read with pleasure by a man as steeped in literature as Robert Schumann himself is evidence that they met at least minimum poetical standards of the day.

SEIT ICH IHN GESEHEN

Seit ich ihn gesehen, glaub' ich blind zu sein;
Wo ich hin nur blicke, seh' ich ihn allein;
Wie im wachen Traume schwebt sein Bild mir vor,
Taucht aus tiefstem Dunkel heller, heller nur empor.

Sonst ist licht und farblos alles um mich her,
Nach der Schwestern Spiele nicht begehr' ich mehr,
Möchte lieber weinen, still im Kämmerlein;
Seit ich ihn gesehen, glaub' ich blind zu sein.

ER, DER HERRLICHSTE VON ALLEN

Er, der Herrlichste von allen,
Wie so milde, wie so gut!
Holde Lippen, klares Auge,
Heller Sinn und fester Mut.

So wie dort in blauer Tiefe,
Hell und herrlich, jener Stern,
Also Er an meinen Himmel,
Hell und herrlich, hehr und fern.

Wandle, wandle deine Bahnen,
Nur betrachten deinen Schein,
Nur in Demut ihn betrachten,
Selig nur und traurig sein!

Höre nicht mein stilles Beten,
Deinem Glücke nur geweiht;
Darfst mich, nied're Magd, nicht kennen,
Hoher Stern der Herrlichkeit!

Nur die Würdigste von allen
Darf beglücken deine Wahl,
Und ich will die Hohe segnen
Viele tausend Mal.

Will mich freuen dann und weinen,
Selig, selig bin ich dann,
Wollte mir das Herz auch brechen,
Brich, o Herz, was liegt daran?

ICH KANN'S NICHT FASSEN

Ich kann's nicht fassen, nicht glauben
Es hat ein Traum mich berückt;
Wie hätt' er doch unter allen
Mich Arme erhöht und beglückt?

Mir war's, er habe gesprochen:
"Ich bin auf ewig dein,"
Mir war's ich träume noch immer,
Es kann ja nimmer so sein.

O laß im Traume mich sterben,
Gewieget an seiner Brust,
Den seligen Tod mich schlürfen
In Tränen unendlicher Lust.

DU RING AN MEINEM FINGER

Du ring an meinem Finger,
Mein goldenes Ringelein,
Ich drücke dich fromm an die Lippen,
An das Herze mein.

Ich hatt' ihn ausgeträumet,
Der Kindheit friedlich schönen Traum,
Ich fand allein mich, verloren
Im öden unendlichen Raum.

Du Ring an meinem Finger,
Da hast du mich erst belehrt,
Hast meinem Blick erschlossen des Lebens
Unendlichen, tiefen Wert.

Ich will ihm dienen, ihm leben,
Ihm angehören ganz,
Hin selber mich geben und finden verklärt mich,
Und finden verklärt mich in seinem Glanz.

HELFT MIR, IHR SCHWESTERN

Helft mir, ihr Schwestern, freundlich mich schmücken,
Dient der Glücklichen heute, mir.
Windet geschäftig mir um die Stirne
Noch der blühenden Myrte Zier.

Als ich befriedigt, freudigen Herzens,
Sonst dem Geliebten im Arme lag,
Immer noch rief er, Sehnsucht im Herzen,
Ungeduldig den heutigen Tag.

Helft mir, ihr Schwestern, helft mir verscheuchen
Eine törichte Bangigkeit;
Daß ich mit klarem Aug' ihn empfange,
Ihn die Quelle der Freudigkeit.

Bist, mein Geliebter, du mir erschienen,
Gibst du mir, Sonne, deinen Schein?
Laß mich in Andacht, la mich in Demut,
Laß mich verneigen dem Herren mein.

Streuet ihm, Schwestern, streuet ihm Blumen
Bringet ihm knospende Rosen dar.
Aber euch, Schwestern, grüß' ich mit Wehmut,
Freudig scheidend aus eurer Schar.

SÜSSER FREUND

Süsser Freund, du blickest mich verwundert an,
Kannst es nicht begreifen, wie ich weinen kann;
Laß der feuchten Perlen ungewohnte Zier
Freudig hell erzittern in dem Auge mir.

Wie so bang mein Busen, wie so wonnevoll!
Wüßt' ich nur mit Worten, wie ich's sagen soll;
Komm und birg dein Antlitz hier an meiner Brust,
Will ins Ohr dir flustern alle meine Lust.

Weißt du nun die Tränen, die ich weinen kann,
Sollst du nicht sie sehen, du geliebter, geliebter Mann?
Bleib' an meinem Herzen, fühle dessen Schlag,
Daß ich fest und fester nur dich drucken mag.

Hier an meinem Bette hat die Wiege Raum,
Wo sie still verberge meinen holden Traum;
Kommen wird der Morgen, wo der Traum erwacht,
Und daraus dein Bildnis mir entgegen lacht!

AN MEINEM HERZEN

An meinem Herzen, an meiner Brust,
Du meine Wonne, du meine Lust!
Das Glück ist die Liebe, die Lieb' ist das Glück,
Ich hab's gesagt und nehm's nicht zurück.

Hab' überschwenglich mich geschätzt,
Bin überglücklich aber jetzt.

Nur die da saügt, nur die da liebt das Kind,
Dem sie die Nahrung gibt nur eine Mutter weiß allein,

Was lieben heißt und glücklich sein.
O wie bedaur' ich doch den Mann,
Der Mutterglück nicht fühlen kann!

Du lieber, lieber Engel, du
Du schauest mich an und lächelst dazu!

NUN HAST DU MIR DEN ERSTEN SCHMERZ GETAN

Nun hast du mir den ersten Schmerz getan,
Der aber traf.
Du schläfst, du harter, unbarmherz'ger Mann,
Den Todesschlaf.
Es blicket die Verlass'ne vor sich hin,
Die Welt ist leer,
Geliebet hab' ich und gelebt, ich bin
Nicht lebend mehr.
Ich zieh' mich in mein Inn'res still zurück,
Der Schleier fällt,
Da hab' ich dich und mein verlor'nes Glück,
Du meine Welt!

SINCE I HAVE SEEN HIM

Since I have seen him, I believe I am blind;
Anywhere I look, I see only him;
As in a waking dream, his image floats before me,
Rising from deepest darkness, brighter, brighter
and ever upward.

Everything else around me is less light and colorful,
My sisters' games no longer appeal to me,
I would rather weep silently in my little room;
Since I have seen him, I believe I am blind.

HE, THE MOST GLORIOUS OF ALL

He, the most glorious of all,
How kind he is, how good!
Sweet mouth, clear eye,
Bright mind and firm courage.

Even as in that blue depth yonder,
That star shines bright and glorious,
So is he in my heaven,
Bright and glorious, sublime and far away.

Wander. wander along your course.
Only to look at your light,
Only to look at it humbly,
Only to be blissful and sad!

Do not hear my silent prayer,
Consecrated to your happiness;
You must not know me, lowly girl,
Noble star of glory!

Only the worthiest of all
May your choice make happy,
And I will bless the noble one,
Many thousand times.

I shall rejoice and I shall weep then,
Blissful, blissful I will be,
Even though my heart should break,
Break, heart, what does it matter

I CANNOT GRASP, NOR BELIEVE IT

I cannot grasp, nor believe it,
A dream must have me bewitched.
How could he from among all others
Have exalted and blessed poor me?

It seemed to me that he had spoken:
"I am forever yours."
I seemed still to be dreaming,
For this can never be.

Oh let me die in my dream,
Cradled on his breast,
Let me drink blissful death
In tears of infinite joy.

YOU RING ON MY FINGER

You ring on my finger,
My little golden ring,
I press you devoutly to my lips,
To this heart of mine.

I had dreamed out
Childhood's peaceful, lovely dream,
I found myself lonely and lost
In empty, infinite space.

You ring on my finger,
You only taught me then,
You opened to my eyes,
Life's infinite, profound worth.

I want to serve him, live for him,
Wholly belong to him
Give myself and find myself
Radiant in his luster.

HELP ME, MY SISTERS

Help me, my sisters, cheerfully adorn me,
Serve me, the happy one, today.

Busily wind around my forehead
The lovely wreath of flowering myrtle.

When I, contented, with a joyful heart,
Earlier lay in my beloved's arms,

He always summoned, his heart filled with longing,
Impatient, this very day.

Help me, my sisters, help me
Cast out a foolish anxiety,
That I with clear gaze may receive him,
Him, the source of all happiness.

Have you, my beloved, appeared to me,
Do you, sun, give me your light?
Let me devoutly. let me humbly,
Let me bow to my master and lord.

Strew, sisters, strew flowers before him,
Offer budding roses to him.
But you, sisters, I greet with sadness,
Joyfully parting from among you.

SWEET FRIEND

Sweet friend, you look amazed at me,
You cannot understand how I can weep;
Let the moist pearl's unaccustomed adornment
With joyful clarity tremble in my eyes.

How frightened is my heart, how filled with rapture,
If only I knew the words with which to tell you;
Come and hide your face here on my breast,
Let me whisper all my delight in your ear.

Now do you understand the tears that I can shed,
Should you not then see them, you beloved, beloved man?

Stay near my heart, feel its throbbing,
So that I may clasp you still firmer and firmer.

Here by my bed the cradle will have its place,
Where it may in silence hide my lovely dream;

There will come a morning when the dream ends,
And from the cradle your likeness will smile up at me!

ON MY HEART, ON MY BREAST

On my heart, on my breast,
You my delight, you my joy!
Happiness is love and love is happiness,
I have said it and won't take it back.

I thought myself so rapturous,
But I am more than happy now,
Only she who suckles, only she who loves the child
To whom she gives nourishment; only a mother can know,
What it means to love and be happy.

Oh, how sorry I am for the man,
Who cannot feel a mother's bliss.
You dear, dear angel you,
You look at me and you smile at me!

NOW YOU HAVE CAUSED ME THE FIRST PAIN

Now you have caused me the first pain,
But it hurt.
You sleep, you hard and cruel man,
The sleep of death.
The now forsaken woman stares into space,
The world is empty, empty.
I have loved and I have lived,
I do not live any more.
I silently withdraw into myself,
The veil is falling,
Then I have you and my lost happiness,
You, my world!

There is a ninth poem in the original cycle, not set by Schumann and therefore not examined here, in which the narrator talks to her granddaughter on the eve of the latter's marriage. Having offered the girl her advice and her blessing, she now awaits her own death with equanimity. Forming a sort of coda, this last poem reinforces the idea of the cyclical nature of women's lives. As we shall see, Schumann accomplishes this purpose less obviously and hence more effectively with a musical coda. There is also one strophe in "Süsser Freund" not included by Schumann.

Naive as he probably was about women when he composed the settings for Chamisso's texts in July of 1840 (three months before his long-delayed marriage to Clara Wieck), Schumann may be forgiven for not rejecting them on the basis of their content. Strong-willed, professionally independent Clara undoubtedly soon enlightened her husband on Chamisso's misapprehensions, but how far off was the poet from the idealized vision of women actually held by most early nineteenth century patriarchs? Certainly total ignorance of sexual matters on the part of their unmarried daughters or fiancées, as implied in "Helft mir, ihr Schwestern," was the goal of most parents and prospective bridegrooms, as was the extreme modesty of speech reflected in "Süsser Freund." Complete absorption in family was a fact for most women of the time and indeed for many subsequent decades, and the overwhelming bliss of motherhood was as yet unquestioned. One may assume that even the exaggerated humility of the young girl in *Frauenliebe und -leben* and the still more exaggerated awe in which she holds her beloved, if not all that universal in reality, would have been generally admired and appreciated by most males in this era of misogynist condescension.

Be that as it may, one is no longer likely to encounter Chamisso's poems without their musical settings, so we shall consider them only as an element—albeit a crucial one—in Schumann's cycle.

One fact which strikes the student of art song is the paucity of large-scale works in the genre that are intended for the female voice. Among the great nineteenth-century German-language cycles, from Beethoven's seminal *An die ferne Geliebte* through

Schubert's *Schöne Müllerin* and *Die Winterreise* and including Schumann's own *Dichterliebe*, only *Frauenliebe und -leben* is appropriately presented by a woman (women have sung *Winterreise* with some success, but it is fairly certain that Schubert envisioned it as interpreted by a man). Even in later French and English-language cycles, those for male voice—Fauré's *La Bonne chanson*, Vaughn Williams' *The House of Life and Songs of Travel*, Benjamin Britten's *Songs and Proverbs of William Blake* or *Holy Sonnets of John Donne* to name but a few—far out number those specifically composed for performance by soprano or contralto, although such works as Fauré's *Chanson d'Eve* or Aaron Copland's *Twelve Poems of Emily Dickinson* are at least as effective when sung by women.

To critics who find *Frauenliebe und -leben* among Schumann's weaker works—and there are many such—its unique availability to the female artist accounts for its continued presence on so many recital programs. (To my knowledge no performance of it by a male singer is recorded in the annals of music history.) Impressed by the total indifference on the part of most audiences to repertoire problems faced by performers, this observer finds it far more likely that the sweetly singable melodies, gently appropriate harmonies, intimate interweaving of vocal line and accompaniment, and tenderly evocative piano postludes with which Schumann graced Chamisso's texts are the factors really responsible for its ongoing popularity.

Schumann gives only one brief introductory measure to the piano before the voice enters. As is so often the case with this composer, the rhythm—simple as it seems—is the key element in the opening phrase, its eighth-note rest interrupting the flow of the music in much the way shyness and uncertainty might cause hesitation in a young girl's speech. The rise in pitch between the top notes of the first two chords, which are semi-detached despite their phrase marks, is a timid, questioning gesture. The singer begins with an echo of the piano's opening phrase, which the piano reiterates in support. At the third measure, Schumann's rhythmic skill becomes even more apparent, as the piano arrives at the high point of the melodic phrase (B flat, the tonic, as analyzed in the key for high voice) on the accented second beat, while the voice pauses, only to echo the B flat one beat later (Ex. I).

Ex. I

Ex. II

Voice and piano complete the first line of text in unison. The strong chord which follows immediately in the accompaniment (it falls on what is ordinarily the weakest place in the measure, the second half of the second beat) serves as a focal point in the modulation as well as a powerful syncopation (Ex. II).

Schumann begins the second line of text with the same music he had given to the first, but this time stated one whole-step higher. Instead of pausing for a brief piano interlude at its conclusion as he had done before, the composer extends the flow of the singer's material to the end of the four-line strophe. Twice within that long outburst of melody the line soars upward, once for "wachen" and once for "Bild" ("waking" and "image"). The stress on "Bild" seems completely warranted, but it might be argued that "Traume" is a more important word in Chamisso's verse than "wachen," which precedes it. Schumann, less concerned with the setting of individual words than, let us say, Schubert, tended to concentrate on the overall mood or sentiment of the text, sometimes at the expense of single words or syllables. Suspensions at "tiefstem" and "Dunkel" create short-lived dissonances between the piano and vocal parts, and just when a tonic resolution seems imminent (at

"empor") Schumann surprises the listener with an altered fifth (the
F# in the piano's bass), extending the music still further, and
leading back to the opening material (Ex. III).

Ex. III

The song is strophic, with only a final tonic chord to prevent the
music from entering a loop from which there is no exit. (Pianists
have nightmares of being unable to extricate themselves from the
equally circular theme of the third movement of Schumann's Piano
Concerto!).

After the tender, yet still tentative, close of "Seit ich ihn
gesehen," the exuberant repeated chords of the accompaniment and
the triadic melodic statement given to the singer at the beginning
of "Er, der Herrlichste von allen" could be interpreted as triumphant as well as passionate. Is Schumann telling us too much too
soon, or is all this energy merely youthful enthusiasm on the
protagonist's part?   All musical elements participate in the
onrushing, rather tempestuous aural picture—the rising octaves in
the piano's bass, the singer's upward ornamental turns at "sie" and
"fester," the abbreviated triadic phrases for the girl's descriptions
of her beloved's attributes ("Holde Lippen, klares Auge"), the
wide rising interval at "heller Sinn"—there's really no stopping this
outburst!

The accompaniment's bass line echoes the singer's figure at
"Holde Lippen" and "klares Auge," overlapping with it to increase
the music's excitement (Ex. I).

Ex. I

When the singer finally pauses at the end of the first strophe, the accompaniment takes up her soaring triadic figure, never for a moment allowing the piece's energy to flag. The sec- ond strophe receives the same musical treatment as the first, save for insignificant adjustments in the vocalist's rhythm to accommodate the words. The piano's interlude at the end of the section is, however, extended to prepare for the new, gentler material to come.

While the music for Strophe III ("Wandle, wandle...") does calm down a bit, it is only at its conclusion that Schumann indicates any slowing of the tempo, and one senses that the girl's excitement is only barely, temporarily contained. As Elaine Brody and Robert Fowkes point out, Chamisso's text leaves us "syntactically stranded" in these lines—we're not sure who or what is doing the wandering.[3]

As we suspected it might, the tumultuous energy of the beginning of the song returns in Strophe IV ("Höre nicht mein stilles Beten..."). The first two lines are yet another repeat of the music heard for the first halves of Strophes I and II, but Schumann changes the music for the rest of the stanza. He repeats the words "hoher Stern der Herrlichkeit," giving a small melisma to the word "Stern" for added emphasis, and brings the strophe to a full close on the tonic.

Even now there is no real letup in the driving energy of the piece, for the piano pushes forward during the singer's brief pause. The climax of the fifth strophe—and the highest note in the song—occurs on the word "Wahl" (choice, selection) as the excited young lady tells the man she loves (one assumes that he is not actually present) that she hopes his choice of mate will make him blissfully happy, even though she knows it cannot be anyone as humble and insignificant as herself. There is a general tapering off after this high point, with descending pitch levels and a ritard at the brave but sad words "brich, o Herz, was liegt daran?"

Quite clearly Schumann does not wish to leave this song on a depressed note, so he repeats the first strophe, as always giving the first two lines their characteristic triadic material, and ending the duet part of the song (for the pianist has been a full partner all the way through) the same way he had concluded Strophe IV, complete with the repeated last line of text. Once again, as is so often the case with Schumann, the piano has the last word in this piece, and, interestingly enough, the composer here introduces completely new material. The effect of the surprisingly complex, partially contrapuntal postlude is both wistful and soothing. The intertwining horizontal strands of its middle measures, which may represent the multiple states of mind of the protagonist, yield to the tender reverie of the extended suspension, under which a rising chromatic line flows in preparation for the final tonic chord (Ex. II).

Ex. II

In many ways the overall tone of Schumann's setting for "Er, der Herrlichste von allen" is unexpected: instead of the reverential awe the protagonist feels for the paragon of male virtues with whom she has fallen love, a sentiment the words spell out clearly enough, the music gives us energetic bravado; instead of the sadness of the self-sacrifice she says she is ready to endure, we

hear her excitement and exaltation. The hints of melancholy found
in the music at "brich, o Herz, was liegt daran?" and in the
postlude are brief, and can hardly be said to reflect real depth of
emotion. Perhaps Schumann, who was usually so adroit at sensing
the emotional import of a poem and then portraying it in musical
terms, felt that the young woman in question knew she need not
despair even this early in the story, although there is no reason to
assume this from Chamisso's text. In any case the upbeat energy
of the song provides a welcome musical contrast to "Seit ich ihn
gesehen."

Text and music more clearly reflect one another at the beginning
of "Ich kann's nicht fassen," the third song in *Frauenliebe und
-leben.* Here we find genuine surprise and delight, as the girl tells
us of her incredible good fortune. The minor tonality, non-legato
melodic line and disconnected accompanying chords of the opening
(Ex. I) reflect the girl's wonderment at her own bliss,

Ex. I

and the music's uneasy resting-place on a diminished harmony
(bars 7-8 in Ex. I) leads the listener to believe that she still has
doubts that her happiness is real. In a recitative of slowly climbing
pitches, heard over sustained chords, the girl sings the verses
beginning "Mir war's" (It seems to me) as though in a trance. To
emphasize her doubt, Schumann has her repeat the words "Es kann
ja nimmer so sein"—It can never be so. Once again an eight-bar
unit, composed of a non-legato melodic line and disconnected
chords similar to those of the beginning, ends on a disquieting
diminished harmony. The music for "in Tränen unendlicher Lust"

which also features a long diminished chord, is slow (the composer writes *Adagio*) and apprehensive.

The *a tempo* instruction at the end of the original poem's last line of text announces a strophic restatement of Chamisso's first stanza. As it had the first time, the music for these four lines ends quietly, after a ritard, on a tonic (C minor for high voice) chord. The ensuing coda, in the form of a postlude in which the voice eventually joins the piano, for a final reiteration of the first two lines of text gives the piano some new material. As he did in the previous song, Schumann uses this added segment to change the mood, for the piano solo is gay and dance-like, uninterrupted by ominous pauses and undisturbed by diminished harmonies. In Schubertian style, Schumann finally moves from the pervasive minor modality to a long, soothing, contented C major broken triad. Apparently the girl, now that her song is over, has at last come to trust in her happiness.

The fourth song in the cycle, "Du Ring an meinem Finger," has one of the loveliest, most singable melodies in the song literature. Like so many of Schumann's tunes, it flows in a circular manner, its end leading naturally back to its beginning. As such, it is the perfect musical analogue for the symbol of which it sings, the ring, the time-honored emblem of marriage.

Ex. I

It is a characteristic of many Schumann songs that the vocal line seems to grow out of the rich piano part which, in many cases, can stand on its own as a piano solo. In *Frauenliebe und -leben* this is especially true of "Du Ring an meinem Finger" and, in a quite different manner, of "Helft mir, ihr Schwestern," the song that follows.

For "Du Ring"'s first eight bars of music, to which are set the first two lines of text, the upper voice of the piano is in unison with the singer's melodic line. A flowing broken-chordal pattern provides rich, pleasant harmonic background to the *Innig* ("heartfelt") melody (Ex. I).

Contrasting material, pleasant but far less memorable than the principal theme, is used for the next stanza, and here the piano is more of an accompanist than a full partner. When Chamisso repeats his opening line of text (beginning of Strophe III), Schumann goes back to his own original material, continuing the musical repeat for the entire third strophe. The tempo begins to quicken at "Ich will ihm dienen," as rising melodic line and agitated chords reflect the tensions the young woman must feel as she pledges to serve her husband in the role of wife, a role as yet mysterious and perhaps a little frightening to her. The musical climax of the piece is on the word "ganz"—"whole, complete, total"—which comes at the end of the second line of the last strophe. Schumann then uses the final two lines of text to calm the music down. To bring the piece full circle to its original mood, Schumann repeats Chamisso's opening stanza to his original setting, with but a slight alteration at the end to make a definite close. In this song the piano postlude introduces neither new material nor contrasting moods.

Schumann has been very deliberate in his establishment of key relationships for the songs of this cycle. Beginning in B flat, he proceeds in the second song to the subdominant (E flat), sets the third song in the subdominant's relative minor (C) and then returns to the E flat subdominant for "Du Ring." (The modulation to C major at the end of "Ich kann's nicht fassen" should not throw us off the scent, for the piece is considered to be in C minor.) The composer now moves back to B flat for the fifth song, "Helft mir, ihr Schwestern," completing one harmonic circle. This circular approach to key relationships is of course totally appropriate to the cyclical nature of both the form and the subject matter of *Frauenliebe und -leben*.

Like "Er, der Herrlichste von allen," "Helft mir, ihr Schwestern" is full of driving, rhythmic energy. The piano is given two
bars in which to establish its characteristic figure: an ascending
tonic triadic pattern answered by a similar descending broken--
chordal group on the relative minor. The dynamism of the pattern
is vastly enhanced by the dotted-eighth-sixteenth-note subdivision
at the end of each measure (Ex. I). This figure is repeated under
much of the vocal line and, in characteristic Schumann fashion,
serves as a unifying factor for the entire piece.

Immer mit Pedal.

Ex. I

The singer enters with an energetic, upward-reaching melody of
her own, for the second half of which she is joined by the upper
voice of the piano part. Despite the exuberant rising interval at
"mich schmücken," the vocal line concludes with the same low
note (F, the dominant) on which it started. Schumann repeats the
four bars to which he has set the first two lines of text for lines
three and four. A more consistently rising melody, rhythmically
enhanced by insistent syncopations in the piano's bass line, invokes
the impatience the protagonist knows her betrothed feels for this
day of fruition and consummation (she can, of course, admit to no
such feelings).

Chamisso's repeat of the words "Helft mir, ihr Schwestern"
brings back Schumann's opening music, to which we now hear the
third strophe sung. Another contrasting section, similar in melodic
content to that of "Als ich befriedigt" but accompanied by agitated
chords, gets us through the obsequious words "Lass mich
verneigen dem Herren mein," which Schumann turns into an
exultant, triumphant, climactic highpoint. This is another example
of his concentrating on the overall message of the text rather than
on any individual phrases or thoughts within it.

For the last stanza of the poem, Schumann begins to reiterate his characteristic "A" music (the song may be schematized, using one symbol for each two lines of text, as A/A//B/B'//A/A//C/C'// A/D//Coda), but this time using the by now familiar theme for only the first half of the strophe. Then, suddenly, a ritard and a drop in dynamics bring a change in mood—the energetic, youthful exuberance is gone. An *a tempo* at the rising melody for the penultimate line of text seems to presage a return to the original spirit of the piece; but no, another ritard and a slowly descending tonic triad bring the singer's part to a subdued conclusion. A piano postlude, its music clearly derived from the principal vocal line of the song and yet eerily suggestive of the Wedding March from Wagner's *Lohengrin* (which of course had not yet been written), brings the song to a solemn, quasi-religious conclusion. The church ceremony has begun.

Early nineteenth-century *pudeur* prevents the poet from mentioning the young couple's new erotic relationship, but in "Süsser Freund" it gives us incontrovertible evidence that the marriage has at least been consummated, for the protagonist is pregnant. Her difficulty in conveying this message to her husband is hard to accept in our era of unblushing public discussion of the most private matters, but Chamisso's view of the scene may very well have been true, at least for the more modest women of his time.

An interesting rhythmic figure, consisting of a rest or a weak end-of-the-phrase note on the ordinarily strong beat of a measure, followed by a phrase begun by a half-note, becomes the characteristic and hence unifying factor of Schumann's setting for "Süsser Freund" (Ex. I).

This arrangement of beats makes for an arresting syncopation, perhaps analogous to the shy wife's attempts to capture her husband's attention as he is about to turn away. Piano and voice often overlap, as the syncopated phrase, beginning impatiently, intrudes on the ending of the previous statement (see measure 4 of Ex. I). Harmonic suspensions such as the chord immediately preceding the voice's entrance (the dominant and tonic played simultaneously) tend to increase the aura of tension, which is somewhat dissipated by the slow tempo suggested by the composer (*Langsam, mit innigen Ausdruck,* slow with heart-felt expression). This is, in fact, the slowest of the eight songs in the cycle.

Ex. I

Ex. II

Schumann sets the first two stanzas of Chamisso's poem to identical music. More or less as he had in the previous song, he uses the material given in the opening line twice, and then completes the strophe with non-repeated contrasting music (A/A/B/C// A/A/B/C is the scheme for the first two strophes). A text-book series of dominant-sevenths then prepares the listener and the husband for the protagonist's announcement, which is delivered in most circumspect terms. The accompaniment becomes a quiet series of semi-detached chords which might have been used to convey mounting excitement, but no increase in tempo indicating such a desire on the part of the composer is indicated. Instead we have a warm, cello-like countermelody in the bass register of the keyboard (Ex. II).

At the introduction to the section in which the wife urges the husband to press his head against her throbbing heart, a *lebhafter*

(livelier) indication over a brand new melody, begun by the piano
alone and later becoming a duet for voice and piano, brings new
animation to the song. In the presentation of this material we see
one of Schumann's signature gestures—a melody begun by the
instrument and completed by the voice (Ex. III).

Ex. III

As the wife clasps her husband to her breast "fest und fester"
(firmly and more firmly: Schumann repeats these words), a rising
melodic line and agitated accompanying chords, played and sung
with increasing animation and dynamic energy, are used to connote
her mounting excitement and joy. A piano interlude calms things
down in preparation for a repeat of the music heard at the
beginning (the overall plan of the song is ternary, the traditional
ABA song form). Once again a postlude follows the conclusion of
the vocal part, but this time, in another characteristic Schumann
gesture, the voice repeats the most significant words of its last line,
"dein Bildnis" (your likeness), over the piano's final chords
(Ex.IV).

Ex. IV

The harmonic relationship of "Süsser Freund" to "Helft mir, ihr
Schwestern," the song that precedes it, is somewhat complex.
"Süsser Freund" is in G major; G minor, that key's parallel, is the
relative minor of B flat, the key of "Helft mir, ihr Schwestern."
The move from "Süsser Freund" to "An meinem Herzen," on the
other hand (from G to D, its dominant), could not be more simple
or more ordinary. A pair of dominant-seventh chords introduces
the new key with as little ado as possible, and the new mood of
"heart-felt gaiety" (*Frölich, innig*) is established thereafter by the
exuberantly rising melodic line and the energetic accompanying
figure (Ex. I).

Ex. I

"An meinem Herzen" is in modified strophic form, with the first
two bars of the song proper (after the introductory chords)
repeated at the beginnings of each of its four strophes. There is
some minor alteration at the end of the characteristic theme to
accommodate differences in the music for the second halves of the

stanzas. A diminuendo and a ritard at the end of Strophe II as well as a move to the treble clef for the accompaniment, whose lowest notes are now above the singer's tessitura, set the stage for some tenderness as the protagonist says that only she who nourishes the baby from her own breast can know the love a mother feels.

The *a tempo* indication at the beginning of the third strophe is somewhat contradicted by the German marking which says *schneller*, faster. At the final strophe the pace is so rapid (*Noch schneller* and *presto*, says Schumann) that the accompaniment must switch to single staccato chords in lieu of its characteristic sixteenth-note figure, and the vocal line is reduced to a galloping abbreviation of its former self. Is this child already a rambunctious toddler the mother must chase, or is it her own inner excitement that carries her away? In either case, the music has all it can do to keep up with her (Ex. II).

Ex. II

Schumann begins a repeat of Chamisso's opening two lines in the same hectic tempo but a ritard toward the end of the first of these two verses signals a slowing-down of activity, and the song ends tenderly. As he has done before in this cycle, Schumann introduces new material and a new mood in the postlude. Marked *langsamer* (slower), this coda is dreamy and wistful. Perhaps, as the child now sleeps, the mother is already picturing the nostalgia she will feel when his early years are over. The final suspension and resolution, so reminiscent of those heard at the end of "Süsser Freund," are perhaps intended to make the listener recall the sweetness of that last "dein Bildnis."

A single chilling D minor chord introduces the last song in *Frauenliebe und-leben*, the sorrowful "Nun hast du mir den ersten Schmerz getan." We have no way of knowing how long the interval has been between the joys of early motherhood as expressed in the penultimate song, and the death of the husband which occasions this final piece; we know only that the widow is angry, resentful, and bereaved. The shift from D major to D minor to indicate the protagonist's move from youthful gaiety to lonely despair is an obvious one.

The widow states her painful thoughts in solemn, dignified recitative, twice moving from the dominant to the tonic and back again in syllabic declamation. Stark chords, all save the dominant A chord under "traf" in the minor mode, accompany her plaint (Ex. I).

Ex. I

Ex. II

A strong dissonance (a diminshed chord with C as its root over a D octave) introduces the next section of text, which is still more declaimed than sung. The accompaniment's rising chords and the singer's B flat to D flat interval on "die Welt ist leer" make an almost painful climax, which Schumann emphasizes with a *sforzando* at the B flat minor chord. Schumann's repetition of the words "ist leer" (empty) increases the pathos of Chamisso's poignant text and gives him time to bring the music down from this dramatic high point (Ex. II).

The rest of the vocal line descends until the voice, hovering around middle C#, sounds flat and deadened. Accompanying chords quietly support the protagonist's *Angst*, until both come to a resting place on an inconclusive dominant (A major) chord. After a long hold, retaining the top note (A) of the piano's chord, Schumann changes the underlying notes to those of an F-7 chord (F/A/C/E flat). This becomes the link between the D minor of the final song and the B flat major postlude, which is a repeat of the first twenty measures of the piano part of the cycle's opening song. It is remarkable how this music, heard at first as a background to a young girl's dream of love, has been transformed by all that has preceded it into a gentle but sad reflection of "A Woman's Love and Life." Its use at beginning and end is a perfect analogue for the cyclical nature of all life, and the particular characteristics of a song cycle as distinct from a group of individual songs.

Notes to Chapter III

1. Robertson, p.395
2. Ibid.
3. Robertson, p.134

CHAPTER IV

BRAHMS

DIE MAINACHT Hölty

Ludwig Heinrich Christoph Hölty (1748-1776) was a member of a group of *literati* from the Hanoverian town of Göttingen. Calling themselves the "Göttinger Hain" (literally the Göttingen Grove or Thicket), these idealistic young writers aimed to promote a feeling of German nationalism through their works. (Despite their efforts Germany was to remain a loosely connected constellation of principalities for a full century after the circa 1770 formation of the Göttenger Hain; it ultimately achieved unification through the Franco-Prussian War of 1870).

Sharing a love of nature and a deep affection for the folklore and songs of the area, the Göttengen poets often wrote in simple elegiac lyric and ode forms. Hölty was probably the most gifted of the group, which included J. M. Miller (1750-1814), J. H. Voss (1751-1826), and the Stolberg brothers, Christian (1748-1821) and F. L. (1750-1819). Hölty retained an echo of the classic Anacreontic style—adaptation or imitation of the Greek poet Anacreon who praised wine, women and song in trochaic tetrameter[1]—even as his poetry became more dreamily melancholic, more for the purpose of "the cultivation and enjoyment of an indistinct mood,"[2] more filled with passive sentiment—in short more pre-Romantic.

DIE MAINACHT

Wann der silberne Mond durch die Gesträuche blinkt,
Und sein schlummerndes Licht über den Rasen streut,

Und die Nachtigall flötet
Wandl' ich traurig von Busch zu Busch.

Überhüllet vom Laub girret ein Taubenpaar
Sein Entzücken mir vor; aber ich wende mich,
Suche dunklere Schatten,
Und die einsame Träne rinnt.

Wann, o lächelndes Bild, welches wie Morgenrot
Durch die Seele mir strahlt, find ich auf Erden dich?
Und die einsame Träne
Bebt mir heisser die Wang' herab.

THE MAYNIGHT

When the silvery moon gleams through the shrubs,
And scatters its slumbering light over the lawn,
And the nightingale sounds like a flute,
I walk sadly from bush to bush.

Under cover of the foliage, a pair of doves
Coo their delight to me; but I turn away,
Looking for darker shadows,
And the lonely tear flows.

When, oh laughing image, that like dawn
Shines through my soul, when shall I find you on earth?
And the lonely tear
Trembles hotter down my cheek.

All the tropes of pre-Romantic German poetry previously
encountered in the Schubert-Rellstab "Ständchen"—the silvery
moonlight, the trilling nightingale, the vague melancholy of the
lonely poet, the delight in nature despite the implicit comparison
between the happy doves and the sad protagonist, the search for
the cover of the forest's dark shadows, and above all the non-spe-
cific yearning—are present in this poem.

Undoubtedly one of his loveliest lyrics, this Hölty piece differs from the simple elegies usually associated with the Göttinger group, for it is in fact written in the highly complex pattern preferred by the Greek poet Asclepiades. According to Asclepiades' design, each line of the poem begins with a strong beat followed by a weak, and then continues strong/weak/weak/strong. The first two verses of each stanza are longer than the other two, and they continue thus: strong/weak/weak/strong/weak/strong; line three adds one weak beat to the shared pattern, and line four concludes with the added weak plus one final strong beat. Below is the Asclepiadic pattern in schematized form.

```
— ⌣ — ⌣⌣ — ‖ — ⌣⌣ — ⌣ —
— ⌣ — ⌣⌣ — ‖ — ⌣⌣ — ⌣ —
— ⌣ — ⌣⌣ — ⌣
— ⌣ — ⌣⌣ — ⌣ —
```

Like its Greek ancestors, Hölty's poem is unrhymed. Its second stanza, omitted in the Brahms setting and hence treated here only in passing, says rather coyly that the poet esteems the fluting nightingale because the latter's little wife lives with him in one nest and gives her singing spouse a thousand cozy kisses. The twice-heard "die einsame Träne," the lonely tear (Strophe II, line four, and Strophe III, line three, as the poem is here presented), is also a bit precious, and the word order of the second line in the final quatrain ("find ich auf Erden dich" instead of the more usual "find ich dich auf Erden") is clearly a necessary accommodation to the difficult asclepiadic meter. According to Brody and Fowkes (*The German Lied and its Poetry*, p. 228), there are several archaisms in the original poem which have been changed in the version used by Brahms (*geusst* instead of *streut* in line two, for example), but since modern anthologies do not show Hölty's earlier choices, we shall not dwell on them.

Brahms' music for "Die Mainacht" (Opus 43 #2), the best-known of his seven Hölty settings (six for solo voice, one for vocal duet), is of unsurpassed beauty. Like his lighthearted "Vergebliches Ständchen," which we shall next discuss, his delightfully romantic "Liebeslieder Waltzes" for piano-duet and quartet of singers, his swashbuckling "Hungarian Dances" (originally for

piano duet and then orchestrated) and so many other pieces one
might name, this lushly expressive song belies Brahms' reputation
as a dour, dark, gloomy composer.   Indeed, "Die Mainacht"
invites performers and listeners alike to enjoy the sensual beauty
of the moonlit scene as they empathize with the gentle melancholy
of the protagonist.

Ex. I

After a two-measure introduction which serves to establish the
key (E flat major in the original, F# for high voice), the 4/4 tempo
and the accompaniment's characteristic division thereof, the singer
enters with a syllabic setting of Hölty's words.   The complex
strong-weak alternations of the asclepiadic metric plan are perfectly
reflected in the music for the entire first strophe (Ex. I).

The singer's first complete phrase ends on a descending major
triad. Although this tonic triad is somewhat veiled by the accompanying harmony, the combination of step-wise and triadic melodic
intervals, characteristic of much of Brahms' vocal writing is
clearly in evidence. The melodic line rises as the words describe
the fluting nightingale, descending again to the tonic to complete
the stanza. The accompaniment follows the rise and fall of the
melodic line with rich harmonic support.

A brief piano interlude effectively separates the first two stanzas, as it prepares for a change of key, piano-figuration and mood. The quietly played semidetached chords, which move back and forth from the new tonic to its adjacent diminished, are like a conspiratorial whisper under the singer's description of the two doves hidden in the foliage (Ex. II).

Ex. II

The music then gathers force, breaking the text after what is admittedly the completed thought of the doves cooing for the poet ("Überhüllet vom Laub girret ein Taubenpaar / Sein Entzücken mir vor"), but in so doing breaking the asclepiadic mold.

The piano's brief interlude, with which the vocal part overlaps, is Brahms at his most rhapsodic, making of these few measures a wonderfully climactic moment (Ex. III).

Ex. III

As the protagonist seeks darker shadows ("Suche dunklere Schatten") the music becomes less impassioned, the singer's

melodic line falling, the piano's soaring broken triads heard no
more. A dominant chord prepares for the return of the original
key and piano figure, but we are not quite yet at the actual repeat
of this modified A / B/ A song. Before the recapitulation a semi-
chromatic ascent in the vocal part takes us to a secondary climax
on the first syllable of the sad word "Träne" (tear). To bring us
down from this high point Brahms allots four long notes to that one
syllable, breaking his heretofore almost exclusively syllabic
practice (the first syllable of "dunklere" is sung on two notes, but
this half-step appoggiatura-and-resolution is far less noticeable).

Fittingly enough, after a piano interlude the poem's final strophe
begins with a recapitulation of the music given to the opening
lines. Once again the setting for the first two lines is in total
accord with the meter of Hölty's ode, but, since Brahms chooses
to repeat the music he has already given to "Und die einsame
Träne," complete with long descending triad on "Träne," when
that phrase reoccurs, the asclepiadic pattern is again lost. Now
Brahms himself opts to repeat a word—"heißer," or hotter—thus
changing the last line to "Bebt mir heißer, heißer die Wang'
herab." To further extend the musical phrase, he gives two
quarter-notes to the first syllable of the second "heißer." The
music reaches two impassioned climaxes in this brief final
section—one on "Träne" and another on the reiterated "heißer."
The choice of "hotter" for the emphasis of repetition changes more
than the meter of the poem, for its doubling seems to lend more
reality to the poet's suffering.

As one critic put it, "Brahms' admiration for Hölty's poetry
notwithstanding, the delicate, sensitive verse of that gentle, shy
youth cannot compete with the rich sentiment and expressivity of
Brahms' song style."[3] That may very well be true, but then no
contest seems to have been intended. The power and beauty of the
new entity created by the combination of Hölty's somewhat pallid
verses and Brahms' impassioned music is undeniable.

VERGEBLICHES STÄNDCHEN
From the folklore of the Lower Rhineland

The delightful little dialogue poem we are about to consider may
have been written in medieval times by one Anton Wilhelm

Florentin von Zucsalmaglio,4 or it may have just developed, as so
many traditional folksongs did, through the embellishments of
generations of anonymous authors. In any case the version of it
set by Brahms, which is known to have existed since the fifteenth
century, may be found in the collection of German-language folk-
poetry known as *Des Knaben Wunderhorn.*

Des Knaben Wunderhorn was compiled by poets L. A. von
Arnim (1781-1831), Clemens Maria Brentano (1778-1842) and J.
J. von Gorres (1776-1848), who were then associated with a group
of writers living in Heidelberg (Brentano and Arnim later moved
to Berlin). Published under their aegis in 1805-8, the work had
both immediate and long-range effects of great importance to
German music and literature. First, it stimulated the interest of the
German people in their own history and oral tradition, some of
which was made available in convenient printed form for the first
time by the Heidelberg set. (Both the Grimm brothers were at one
time involved with the Heidelberg circle, and more than a little of
what the latter's research uncovered found itself into the Grimms's
stories.) So strong was the patriotic sentiment aroused by *Des
Knaben Wunderhorn,* in fact, that many historians give the
collection at least partial credit for stimulating the 1813 uprisings
against Napoléon I.[5]

More important to our study is the fact that so many of the
poems printed in the anthology have been used as texts for musical settings. Mahler alone wrote 23 songs to *Des Knaben Wunderhorn* poems and also incorporated several of them into his second,
third and fourth symphonies; composers as different from one
another as Robert Schumann and Arnold Schoenberg have been
inspired by these Volkslied as have Mendelssohn, Richard Strauss,
and, of course, Brahms, who set "Vergebliches Ständchen," his
Opus 84 #4, in 1868.

VERGEBLICHES STÄNDCHEN

> (Er.) Guten Abend, mein Schatz,
> Guten Abend, mein Kind,
> Ich komm' aus Lieb' zu dir,
> Ach, mach' mir auf die Tür!

(Sie.) Mein Tür ist verschlossen,
Ich lass' dich nicht ein.
Mutter, die rät mir klug,
Wärst du herein mit Fug,
Wär's mit mir vorbei!

(Er.) So kalt ist die Nacht,
So eisig der Wind,
Dass mir das Herz erfriert,
Mein' Lieb' erlöschen wird;
Öffne mir, mein Kind!

(Sie.) Löschet dein' Lieb',
Lass sie löschen nur!
Löschet die, immerzu,
Geh' heim zu Bett, zur Ruh',
Gute Nacht, mein Knab'!

A FUTILE SERENADE

(He) Good evening, my sweetheart,
Good evening my child,
I come out of love for you,
Oh, open the door for me!

(She) My door is locked,
I won't let you in.
Mother, who gives me good advice,
[Says] if you come in,
It would all be over with me!

(He) The night is so cold,
The wind so icy,
That my heart will freeze,
And my love will be extinguished;
Open for me, my child!

(She) If your love dies,
Let it perish!

Let it perish, never mind;
Go home to bed, to sleep,
Good night, my lad!

Of the many elements contributing to the charm of "Vergebliches Ständchen," not the least is its impishly pert ending. One
assumes the success of the singer of the serenade in most pieces of
the genre, but with the saucy young female of this duo the
impatient young man gets absolutely nowhere. His argument is
comically practical—let me in because it's cold outside; her
response is equally matter-of-fact—then go home. He threatens her
with the freezing of his love for her; she says (and we paraphrase)
if that's the way it is, that's the way it is.

The diction of the poem is simple and colloquial ("Mutter, die
rät mir klug," and "Wär's mit mir vorbei!" for instance), with
short sentences, short phrases and lots of repetition. Irregular
stanza lengths (four lines for the first, five for the others), metric
patterns (two lines of anapests followed by one line of iambs and
one of mixed feet in the first quatrain alone) and rhyme schemes
(A/B /C/C // A/B/C/C/D // A/B/C/C/B // A/B/C/C/D) add to the
conversational, almost anti-literary style of the delightful little
poem.

Brahms' setting immediately captures the jaunty flavor of the
text. In his mood indication, *Lebhaft und gut gelaunt*, he admon-
ishes the performers to be lively and of good cheer, making it
clear that no one is really going to suffer because of the maiden's
dismissal of her would-be lover. The 3/4 rhythm and the ascending triadic pattern he uses for the first half of the melody and
principal accompanying figure convey the lilt of the popular
Viennese Waltz (Brahms is known to have loved the waltzes of
Johann Strauss, once signing an autograph with the opening bars
of "The Blue Danube Waltz" and the phrase "Unfortunately not by
Johannes Brahms").

The first two sections of dialogue—his opening plea and her
explanation for her refusal—are sung to music that is identical
except for some ornamental variations in the accompaniment.
Brahms freely repeats phrases of the text as needed for musical

balance, with no harm done to the integrity of the poem. The idea
of dialogue is extended from that of the two protagonists to the two
performers, for the piano sometimes joins and sometimes antici-
pates the vocalist's melodic line. As is his wont, Brahms writes
his melodies in a combination of step-wise and triadic intervals, but
the prevailing upward nature of most of the melodic movement
keeps the music gay and buoyant (Ex. I).

Ex. I

In the third stanza the lad begins to complain of his plight, out
in the cold night air with the icy wind freezing his heart. For this
not-too subtle argument Brahms uses an equally obvious musical
ploy, switching from the major to the minor mode. This use of
identical musical material, moved so blatantly and so facilely from
the major to the minor, arouses amused disbelief rather than the
pathos clearly desired by the lad. In this third strophe the
accompaniment becomes even busier than in the second section,
with quasi-independently running eighth-notes (they are still
harmonically of a piece with the melody) replacing the unisons of
the opening (Ex. II).

Ex. II

A return to the major mode for the fourth segment of this strophic song assures us that the lass is not at all moved by thoughts of icy winds and frozen loves. As she sends the serenader on his way, the piano plays a bouncy figure partly consisting of triads in contrary motion, to aid and abet her determined stance. Several extra *Gute Nachts* complete her thoughts and the poem, after which the piano polishes things off with an extra rise in the thematic material and a most conclusive final cadence.

MÄDCHENLIED   Paul Heyse

Paul Heyse (1830-1914) was one of the better-known members of a group of literary men with whom King Maximilian II of Bavaria surrounded himself during the two decades preceding the Franco-Prussian War of 1870, the years of his Munich Court's intellectual prime. Most highly regarded for his original works in prose—his novels and above all his short stories—Heyse was also a prolific dramatist, translator of Italian and English literature, and composer of lyric poetry and tales in verse.   In 1910 he was awarded the Nobel Prize for Literature.

MÄDCHENLIED

Auf die Nacht in der Spinnstub'n
Da singen die Mädchen,
Da lachen die Dorfbub'n,
Wie flink gehn die Rädchen!

Spinnt Jedes am Brautschatz,
Dass der Liebste sich freut.
Nicht lange, so gibt
Es ein Hochzeitgeläut.

Kein Mensch der mir gut ist,
Will nach mir fragen;
Wie bang mir zu Mut ist,
Wem soll ich's klagen?

Die Tränen rinnen
Mir übers Gesicht,
Wofür soll ich spinnen?
Ich weiss es nicht!

A MAIDEN'S SONG

At night in the spinning room,
The girls sing,
The guys from the village laugh,
How quickly the wheels turn!

Everyone spins for her dowry,
So her sweetheart will be pleased,
It won't be long now, till
Wedding bells ring.

There's nobody who is fond of me,
Who will ask for me;
How uneasy I am,
To whom shall I complain?

The tears run
Down my face,
Why should I spin?
I do not know!

This is an effective little poem whose progression from a pleasant description of a charming scene to the expression of the narrator's deep sorrow leaves the reader much moved. In keeping with its two moods, the first half of the poem is full of sounds—the hum of the spinning wheel, the singing of the girls, the laughter of the boys, and the ringing of the wedding bells—while its conclusion speaks only of quiet tears and silent loneliness. The poem's diction is simple and if it were not for its end rhymes (A/B/A/B except in the second strophe where the first and third lines do not rhyme) one could easily believe that it was an honest record of the thoughts of a village girl just as she revealed them. The scene is one of village life circa 1850, and the term "Dorfbub'n" (guys from the village) is a village- dialect locution; in fact the only elevated, poetic language associated with this "Mädchenlied" is that found in most song- book translations of it. The poet's use of "da" in the second line of the opening stanza (there the girls are spinning) gives rise to an interesting question: is the narrator of the first half of the poem the protagonist of the second? Since the answer seems to be affirmative, if she herself is not in that room, where is she? Somewhere on the outside, alone.

This Brahms-Heyse "Mädchenlied," the composer's Opus 107 #5, was composed in 1889. It is followed in Brahms' song catalogue only by the *Vier ernste Gesänge (Four Serious Songs)* of 1896 (Op. 121) and a "Regenlied" (WOO) which was published in 1908 but whose date of composition is unkown. It is one of four Heyse settings by this composer, including a second "Mädchen-lied" (Op. 95 #6) which is actually an adaptation by Heyse from an Italian text.

Needless to say, by 1889 Brahms (1833-1897) was a mature and experienced composer of songs. When a text touched him, as this Heyse poem obviously did, he composed music of exquisite pathos for it. In this instance he matched the poet's simplicity and directness, thereby making the emotional content of the text all the more palpable.

Perhaps because virtually all folk-song settings are strophic, Brahms elected to express this village-girl's plaint in modified strophic form. He therefore uses the same music—a simple, primarily syllabic minor-mode melody over a flowing sixteenth-note accompanying figure—for the first three stanzas of verse (Ex. I).

Ex. I

Ex. II

The girl's sadness is immediately apparent in the music: although she describes festive sounds and activities, she in no way shares the youthful gaiety she sees all about her. The unexpected modulation to D major at the word "Dorfbub'n" is characteristic of Brahms' late piano pieces from Opus 116 through Opus 119, and, in fact, the setting as a whole might very well belong to this wonderful group of subtle miniatures. A brief piano interlude of interweaving melodic strands separates the poem's stanzas (Ex. II).

The third verse repeats the music we have heard twice before, but with a somewhat simplified accompaniment at its beginning. This time, however, the interlude which follows ends with a major instead of a minor tonic chord, introducing new material as it changes modality. The accompaniment for this "B" section (the song may be loosely schematized as A/A/A/B, which differs from the poet's basically binary division) begins with a series of broken chords (E major, E minor, diminished, B major) over an ostinato tonic bass note, while the melody, after an initial rising interval, descends with stepwise motion. A brief interlude in the form of a concluding plagal cadence (E minor to B major) reinforces the major modality of this section, but, strangely enough, the mood is in no way lightened by the modal shift.

Ex. III

A sudden *forte*, the first in the song (the mood instruction is *Leise bewegt*, soft and delicate, flowing; the dynamic markings to this point have been *piano, più piano and dolce*), renders all the more powerful the rise to F sharp and the pathetic D sharp minor chord accompanying it. This is the music to which the girl describes her tears. An even stronger chord—a discord made up of an augmented G over a broken E minor—underscores her anguish as she sings "Ich weiss es nicht!" (Ex. III)

Brahms repeats this last pathetic phrase twice, thereby stretching the final two lines of text over twelve bars of music and making them the temporal equivalent of a whole stanza. The first repeat is an echo of the penultimate measures of the first three strophes, the second an exquisitely simple combining of vocal and piano parts as the by-now familiar diminished chord rooted in E is built atop a bass-line F sharp (Ex. IV).

Ex. IV

On the singer's last note, a tonic B, the accompaniment has a B chord used as a dominant seventh, and hence stated with a major third (the D sharp). This has been the beginning of all the principal piano interludes, and the piece does indeed end with yet another repeat of this four-bar passage. Although we have come to expect this piano music, its significance is all the greater in this, its last statement, for it leaves the singer's last phrase—"I do not know!"—unresolved and questioning.

In the first two strophes Brahms ended the interlude in the minor, and for the third he moved to major.   Clearly either modality fits and he has a choice.   Interestingly enough, to end the sad little song he chooses the major.   Is this a note of solace? Perhaps, although this listener is left with the feeling of pathos.

Notes to Chapter IV

1. Babette Deutsch, *Poetry Handbook 4th Edition* (Barnes and Noble, 1981) p.12

2. Menhennet, p. 110

3. Stein, p. 144

4. Brody and Fowkes, p. 248

5. *Encyclopaedia Britannica* 1952 Edition, article on German Literature, pp. 225-6

CHAPTER V

HUGO WOLF

DAS VERLASSENE MÄGDLEIN
text by Eduard Mörike

Because of the "subtle interweaving of thought, mood, emotion, impression and suggestion"[1] in his works, Eduard Mörike (1804-75) has been called "the first great symbolist poet."[2]

A painter, a pastor and a good amateur musician as well as a first class writer, Mörike, who was born in Ludwigsburg, was the most gifted of the so-called Swabian poets who gathered around Ludwig Uhland (1787-1862). Through his duties as a village clergyman, a position he maintained as much through necessity as vocation, Mörike acquired an intimate knowledge of the emotional life of the peasants and other rural folk. Perhaps because of this involvement, and in spite of its "delicate suggestiveness," his verse has been seen as "the quintessence of *Volkslied*."[3]

In contrast to fellow protosymbolists like Baudelaire and Verlaine, Mörike never lost contact with nature, and never came to value the man-made and the artificial over the natural. In his "Septembermorgen," for example, he describes with elegant simplicity a world, veiled by mist when woods and meadows are still dreaming, but awash in the autumnal glory of warm gold when revealed by the blue sky of day. Rather than regarding nature as mere background to man's personal cares and desires, he often makes nature herself the principal protagonist of a poem, in "Um Mitternacht," for instance he speaks of night as though it were human ("Calmly night has disembarked. She leans dreaming against the wall of hills...").

Perhaps the most unusual element in Mörike's output is a 1delightfully irreverent sense of humor, a characteristic notoriously lacking in most Romantic poets, and in German poets in general. In "Pastoralerfahrung" (A Clerical Experience), to

name one example, he reports that his good country folk lead him
a fine dance and ask for a 'powerful sermon': on Saturday night
after eleven they steal the lettuce from his garden; at matins, quite
at their ease, they expect the vinegar for it, but the end of the
sermon must be suitably mild, for they like to get the oil into the
bargain.[4]

Mörike's poetry was first published in volume form in 1838.
Several enlarged editions appeared subsequently, and the edition
owned by Hugo Wolf—the sixth, published posthumously in
1876—contained 275 poems. Wolf composed music for fifty-three
of these Mörike texts, compared with 51 poems by Goethe, 20
each by Heine and Eichendorff and 17 by Lenau, his other principal sources. We shall examine two Wolf-Mörike songs: "Das
Verlassene Mägdlein" and "Begegnung."

DAS VERLASSENE MÄGDLEIN

> Früh, wann die Hähne krähn,
> Eh die Sternlein schwinden,
> Muß ich am Herde stehn,
> Muß Feuer zünden.
>
> Schön ist der Flammen Schein,
> Es springen die Funken;
> Ich schaue so darein,
> In Leid versunken.
>
> Plötzlich, da kommt es mir,
> Treuloser Knabe,
> Daß ich die Nacht von dir
> Geträumet habe.
>
> Träne auf Träne dann
> Stürzet hernieder;
> So kommt der Tag heran
> O ging er wieder!

THE FORSAKEN MAIDEN

Early, when the cocks are crowing,
Before little stars fade,
I must stand at the stove,
I must light the fire.

Lovely is the shining luster of the flames,
The sparks spring up,
I look into them,
Sunk in sorrow.

Suddenly it seems to me,
Faithless boy,
That during the night
I dreamed of you.

Then tear after tear
Falls down;
So the day comes
Oh if only it would go again!

By the time Wolf set "Das verlassene Mägdlein" some fifty settings of that text by other composers had already been published. We know that Wolf was well acquainted with Robert Schumann's version, because he spoke of his own temerity in trying to rival it; if he was aware of any of the others, he was undoubtedly less concerned with them.

What was it that made this particular text so appealing to composers? The description of the young servant girl, up before sunrise to perform her menial tasks, burdened with a sorrow caused by a faithless lover, robbed of the solace of her dreams when day comes and, as the tears blind her eyes, longing for night to fall again, certainly makes a strong appeal to one's sympathies, but is hardly unique or original. What is striking about the poem is the chiarascuro with which the scene is painted, the play of dark and light, the contrast between the little stars and the shining luster of the fire's sparks and flames on the one hand, and the girl's blinding tears on the other. Equally effective is the alternation of movement and repose: the maiden must stand at the stove, but the sparks and flames spring up from the fire she lights; she is sunk in sorrow, but her sudden recollection of her dream brings her to life. That reawakening to the awareness of her sorrow is shortlived, for tears fall down her face as though she has not force enough even actively to cry. Then too there is the warmth of the flames and the girl's dreams played against the coldness of the house at dawn and the truth of her existence. Without a single detail about the actual story, Mörike has painted "a whole world of love and loss."[5]

The poem, originally part of Mörike's novel *Maler Nolten* (Nolten the Painter), is sung by a serving-girl working in a downstairs kitchen and overheard by another character in the book. Its rhyme scheme is an ordinary A/B/A/B and its language is simple and free of poetic circumlocutions. Each stanza begins with a line in dactyllic meter (a strong beat followed by two weak beats) and ends with a dactyl-trochee combination, but verses within the stanzas vary in accentual pattern. Present tense—the customary story-telling tense of *Volkslied*—is used throughout, and there is a general air of passivity.

Hugo Wolf's creative psychological profile may be the strangest in the history of music. Inactive for months and sometimes years at a time, and eventually unable to work at all, he was occasionally seized by an inspiration so strong and so intense that it allowed him no rest until it had burned itself out. During these brief intervals—biographers estimate that they occupied no more than a total of six months' time in his entire forty-three year existence (1860-1903)—he worked in a mad frenzy, unable to eat or sleep until he had put his musical thoughts on paper.[6] Although deeply felt expressions of pain and longing like "Das Verlassene Mägdlein" often moved him to these aesthetic cataclysms, Wolf's 242-song catalogue also includes settings of texts describing "rogues, poets, sailors, hunters, kings, humorists, philosophers, flowers, mountains, clouds, sunsets, dawns, mid-nights, elves, birds, fairy-tale objects and real people,"[7] all of them, including the many humorous ditties, evidently composed with the same diabolical energy.

Wolf's setting for "Das Verlassene Mägdlein," composed in
March 1888 and the seventh of his Mörike songs, is simplicity
itself. Its A/B/C/A structure conforms in outline to the four-
strophe design of the poem, a coincidence emphasized by the significant musical interludes between stanzas. Aside from minor
deviations at the ends of several lines, its vocal part matches the
text note-for-syllable. Jack M. Stein writes: "It was a point of
honor to Hugo Wolf, fervent disciple of Richard Wagner, that the
music of his songs should match the poetic declamation, the word
and sentence accent."[8]

The song begins with a piano introduction whose plaintive,
falling figure comes to dominate the entire piece both rhythmically and melodically (Ex. I).

The key signature was originally A minor, regarded by Wolf as
"wistful and feminine"[9] (our examples are taken from a transposition to G minor) but the actual tonality of the piece remains
ambiguous until the postlude, and, since the final chord is an open
fifth, the modality is never definitively stated. If a non-musical
parallel be sought for this deliberate avoidance of an obvious
tonic-dominant schema, the girl's vaguely suggested story of
seduction and abandonment might qualify.

Ex. I

After the first strophe, which is clearly dominated by the
melancholy minor and which is most effective when sung in a flat,
vibratoless manner, optimistic tonic chords in the major mode
prepare for the stanza in which the maiden speaks of the shining
luster of the fire. The thrice-repeated movement from the tonic to
a seventh based on the median might suggest the erratic leaping of
the sparks and flames (Ex. II).

An exquisite false cadence to the flatted tonic (from "Funken"
to "Ich schaue") introduces a chromatic passage in which we hear
the girl's anguish ever more poignantly expressed (Ex. III).

A series of augmented chords tears at our hearts during the ensuing piano interlude, and continues under the more animated, ever rising and intensifying vocal expression of the third stanza (Ex. IV).

Ex. II

Ex. III

Ex. IV

Chromaticisms and augmented harmonies characterize the gradual calming—or should one say deadening?—of the protagonist's passionate outburst, until a three-bar interlude consisting of a minor, a major and a dominant-seventh chord respectively brings back the original musical material.   The inconclusive ending of the vocal part—it breaks off on the dominant note—would seem to be an analogue for the maiden's cyclical despair, which, having been alleviated by dreams, begins again with the dawning of each new day.   This hopelessness is once again best portrayed by a ghostly but ethereal, almost toneless, vocal quality.

BEGEGNUNG   Mörike

Was doch heut Nacht ein Sturm gewesen,
Bis erst der Morgen sich geregt!
Wie hat der ungebetne Besen
Kamin und Gassen ausgefegt!

Da kommt ein Mädchen schon die Straßen,
Das halb verschüchtert um sich sieht:
Wie Rosen, die der Wind zerblasen,
So unstet ihr Gesichtchen glüht.

Ein schöner Bursch tritt ihr entgegen,
Er will ihr voll Entzücken nahn:
Wie sehn sich freudig und verlegen
Die ungewohnten Schelme an!

Er scheint zu fragen, ob das Liebchen
Die Zöpfe schon zurecht gemacht,
Die heute Nacht im offnen Stübchen
Ein Sturm in Unordnung gebracht.

Der Bursche träumt noch von den Küssen,
Die ihm das süße Kind getauscht,
Er steht, von Anmut hingerissen,
Derweil sie um die Ecke rauscht.

THE MEETING

What a dreadful storm there was last night
Before morning first stirred!
How the uninvited broom
Swept out the narrow streets and chimneys!

Now through the streets a lass comes
Who looks around half intimidated;
Like roses blown around by the wind,
The blush comes and goes from her little face.

A handsome boy comes toward her,
He wants to approach her, full of delight,
With what embarrassed joyful glances
The two inexperienced young rogues meet!

He seems to ask his love
If she's already dressed her braids
Blown into disorder that night
By the stormy wind that swept through her little room.

The youth still dreams of the kisses
Which the sweet child exchanged with him last night,
He stands, enraptured by her charming grace
While she rushes around the corner.

This enchanting poem stands in distinct contrast to the sorrowful Mörike text we have just finished discussing. Whereas in
"Das Verlassene Mägdlein" the poet creates a feeling of hopeless
immobility by the use of heavy-hearted trochees and dactyls, in
"Begegnung" his lively iambs whisk the happy lovers through
windswept streets; whereas in the unspecified woe of the serving
girl we read a deep wound that even time may not heal, in the
subtle but unmistakable references to a night of love in "The
Meeting" we sense unmitigated joy in the here and now.

When the poem opens, the storm, a not uncommon metaphor for
love-making, has passed; nevertheless the primarily single-

syllabled words of the first two lines of text evoke the disjunctive motion of wind-blown rain. We are not just to hear about the storm—we are to some extent to experience it. To those looking for intertextual readings, Mörike's trope of an "ungebetne Besen" (un invited broom) for the wind might bring to mind Goethe's story of the Sorcerer's Apprentice!

Lest we fear some truly cataclysmic event—some *Drang* to go with this *Sturm*—in the second stanza Mörike gives us two diminutive endings, the common *Mädchen* (maiden) and the somewhat unusual *Gesichtchen* (literally "little face"), to bring down the emotional level. Two additional diminutives, the *Liebchen* (sweetheart) and *Stübchen* (little room) found in the fourth strophe, reinforce the feeling that one is hearing a charming but small-scaled story. The many negative prefixes in the poem—*ungebetne, unstet, ungewohnten, Unordnung*—further undercut unduly serious interpretations of the text.

The fact that Mörike never deviates from the usual A/B/A/B rhyme scheme is in itself of no special interest, but the reiteration of the "en" end sound for the first and third lines of all five stanzas, and the use of a final "t" in the second and fourth lines of all but the third strophe are worthy of note. This kind of repetition provides satisfying unity to the text while binding it close to *Volkslied* style.

In his setting of "Begegnung" Wolf has seized upon the Schubertian device of finding a musical equivalent for one element of the text—in this case the wind—and then using that characteristic musical figure throughout the song. This method of composition is particularly apt for the Mörike poem in question, for the wind is present or implied in four of its five stanzas: in the first strophe it is the principal element of the storm; in the second it is used metaphorically in the description of the girl's blushing cheeks; in the fourth it is said to have swept through her little room; and even in the final strophe, where it is not specifically mentioned, the way the young girl rushes around the corner reminds us of the way it had blown that night.

As in Schubert's songs of this nature, in Wolf's "Begegnung" it is up to the instrumental accompaniment to portray the salient feature. This the piano immediately does in a four bar introduc-

tion remarkable for its onomatopoeic depiction of the wind whirling through the streets, in turn swelling and abating in dynamics,
but never diminishing in speed. Wolf deliberately creates harmonic ambiguity in this introduction, beginning the song with a plagal
scale-chord pattern (A flat minor in the original key of E flat major
but G flat minor in the transposition to D major used as illustration
here). It is possible to see this as a musical metaphor for the
confusion caused at first by the stormy wind and later by the
embarrassment of the two young lovers (Ex. I).

Ex. I

Ex. II

When the voice joins the piano for the first stanza, the singer
seems to lead the accompaniment in a whirling-dervish dance,
anticipating by a sixteenth-note the melodic notes in the piano's
treble line (Ex. II). This pattern will be abandoned at the second
stanza, only to return later on during the song.

The music for the first and third verses of the opening stanza
begins with a repeat of the first measure of the introduction and
continues in the same harmonic pattern. The second line ends on
a somewhat reassuring dominant, but the strophe concludes with
an ominous minor tonic harmony. At this point it is still far from
clear what the principal tonality of the song will be, but the
ensuing piano interlude moves us to what will eventually be

recognized as the tonic major. This harmonic change, coupled with a simpler and gentler accompanying figure, creates a new, sunny mood, alleviating the anxiety without, however, diminishing the pace (Ex. III).

Ex. III

Obviously there is still swift movement, but now it is from the girl herself rather than the storm. The blush comes and goes from her little face like roses blown by the wind, says the poet in an image of surpassing sweetness. One cannot associate fear with such a charming sight!

The melodic line for the second stanza is similar to that used in the first, but with the voice and upper line of the piano now in unison. This time, however, the voice carries the upward scale only four degrees, leaving to the accompaniment the delightful task of completing the climb. Interesting clashes at "um sich," "unstet" and "Gesichtchen" spice this otherwise harmonically benign strophe.

Once again Wolf separates the quatrains with a piano interlude and then changes the key, this time (for the third strophe) moving to the dominant. Since we are still in the major mode and rising melodic lines predominate, the atmosphere remains gay as the poet describes the way these "unaccustomed young rogues" exchange "embarrassed joyful glances." The interlude preceding the fourth quatrain, which ends on a seventh chord rooted on the third degree of the tonic scale, takes us back to the ominous minor mode and the original sixteenth-note separation of voice and piano with which the song began. This return seems to be more for musical than textual reasons, for the poem at this point refers to the storm as a thing of the past and hence no longer to be feared. In fact, it is at this point in the text that the tender question the lad "seems" to ask (has she had time to put her braids back in order?) leaves us no doubt that theirs had been a night of happy love-making. But Wolf might not be so far off in placing anxiety among the emotions two brand-new lovers might feel on seeing each other after their first night of love. Discords at "Stübchen" and "Unordnung gebracht" underscore the poet's reference to the "disorder" in the girl's wind-swept little room, but we do not really believe that it was the wind that caused her braids to come undone.

For the final strophe Wolf reunites voice and piano and returns to the happy tonic major tonality. As it had in the previous section in this key and with this simpler accompanying figuration (Strophe II), the voice tends to linger on one note while the piano plays out the scale-based tune, the latter consequently rising above the former in pitch for much of the time. A fade-out postlude, with accelerating motion in the bass notes and an ever-rising melodic line, provides a charming gestural analogue for the end of the poem, when the girl rushes around the corner and out of sight.

According to Eric Sams,[10] Hugo Wolf set "Begegnung" and "Das Verlassene Mägdlein" just two days apart, the former on the 22nd, the latter on the 24th of March, 1888. Two more different, more complementary songs would be hard to imagine, each so effective, each so expressive of the respective poem's import.

Notes to Chapter V

1. Stein, p.155.
2. Eric Sams, *The Songs of Hugo Wolf* (London: Eulenberg Books, 1972, revised edition) p. 62.
3. Robertson, p. 439.
4. The paraphrases of these three poems are based on those in *The Penguin Book of German Verse*, Introduced and edited by Leonard

Forster, 1959.
5. Sams, p. 73.
6. Brody and Fowkes, p. 258.
7. Ibid., p. 260.
8. Stein, p. 163.
9. Sams, p. 74.
10. Ibid., p. 73.

Chapter VI

Richard Strauss

STÄNDCHEN   A. F. von Schack

A. F. von Schack (1815-1894) was one of the lesser-known literary figures who gathered at the Munich court of King Maximilian of Bavaria. His love for exotic literature, a passion shared by other members of the group, is reflected in his translations of works by the Persian poet Abul Qasim Mansur, better known by his *nom de plume*, Firdusi. (The author of the great epic "Shahnama" as well as a long narrative poem retelling the story of Joseph and Potiphar's wife, Firdusi lived from about 940 to about 1020.)

Von Schack was a patron of all the arts and his reputedly splendid picture gallery made his home attractive as a meeting place for Munich cognoscenti. His poems, overlooked by most important composers, obviously had great appeal for Richard Strauss, who from 1885 to 1888 set sixteen of them to music (four of the five songs from Opus 15, the six of Opus 17, of which "Ständchen" is the second, and the six of Opus 19). From August 1886 to July 1889 Strauss was the assistant conductor at the Munich Opera, and one may safely suppose that during those years he was acquainted with the by then elderly von Schack, a circumstance which may have influenced his choice of that poet's texts. In any case the decision to set "Ständchen" was clearly a happy one, for the song has become the most popular piece Strauss contributed to the genre. Indeed so successful is the music per se that other composers have transcribed it for piano solo. piano duet, various chamber ensembles, salon band and full symphony orchestra.

STÄNDCHEN

Mach auf, mach auf, doch leise, mein Kind,
Um Keinen vom Schlummer zu wecken.

Kaum murmelt der Bach, kaum zittert im Wind
Ein Blatt an den Büschen und Hecken.
D'rum leise, mein Mädchen, dass nichts sich regt,
Nur leise die Hand auf die Klinke gelegt,

Mit Tritten, wie Tritte der Elfen so sacht,
Um über die Blumen zu hüpfen,
Flieg' leicht hinaus in die Mondscheinnacht,
Zu mir in den Garten zu schlüpfen.
Rings schlummern die Blüten am rieselnden Bach
Und duften im Schlaf, nur die Liebe ist wach.

Sitz' nieder, hier dämmert geheimnissvoll
Unter den Lindenbäumen,
Die Nachtigall uns zu Häupten soll
Von uns'ren Küssen träumen,
Und die Rose, wenn sie am Morgen erwacht
Hoch glühn von den Wonneschauern der Nacht.

SERENADE

Open up, open up, but softly, my child,
To awaken no one from slumber.
The brook scarcely murmurs, scarcely a leaf
On the bushes and hedges moves in the wind.
Therefore softly, my lass, so that nothing stirs.
Just quietly put your hand on the latch.

With steps like the elves', so cautious,
To skip over the flowers,
Fly lightly out into the moon-shiny night;
Slip to me in the garden.
All about are slumbering, the blossoms at the trickling
brook,
And give off scent in sleep, only love is awake.

Sit down, here it grows mysteriously dusky
Under the linden trees.
The nightingale overhead should

Dream of our kisses,
And the rose, when it awakens in the morning,
Glow hotly from the night's thrills of delight.

The plan of "Ständchen" is somewhat unusual: instead of the
common quatrain, von Schack writes six-verse stanzas, each with
the rhyme scheme A/B/A/B/C/C; instead of rhymes contained
within the sestet, many of the poem's end-sounds echo from stanza
to stanza ("sacht"/"Mondscheinnacht," the ends of the first and
third lines of the second stanza, and "erwacht"/"Nacht," the
rhymed couplet at the end of the final sestet, for example).
"Bach"/"wach," the end-sounds of the couplet concluding the
central strophe, are similar enough to the "sacht"/"Nacht" group
to qualify as further unifying echoes. Then too we have the
repeated "d" or "t" sounds at the ends of so many of the verses in
all three sestets (they are pronounced in identical fashion), as well
as the extensive inner alliteration of the many "k" sounds in the
first sestet.

What is most certainly not unusual about von Schack's poem is
its use of the tropes so typical of this type of lyric: the murmuring
brook, the soft breeze, the moonlit night, the sweet scents, the
dusky woods which provide shelter and privacy, the sleeping rose
and—most indispensible of all—the ubiquitous nightingale.
Although tradition has it that the nightingale stops singing when
love is requited, the particular bird in this "Ständchen" may be an
exception, for the "Sitz nieder, hier..." of the last sestet implies
that the loved one has complied with her serenader's request to
come to him. The final thought, that when the rose-blossom
reopens in the morning she will blush at the memory of the
delights she witnessed during the night, is a slight departure from
the conventions of the serenade, for it assumes that nature will
overtly respond to the lovers' activities.

Despite the fact that the speaker of von Schack's "Ständchen" is
clearly the male of the duo, Strauss' song, with its delicate,
predominantly treble-clef accompaniment, seems at least as suitable
for female singers as for tenors or baritones, and in fact is often
sung by vocally, albeit not necessarily physically, light-weight

coloraturas. The rising dominant octaves and ensuing leap to the tonic which comprise the opening melodic phrases of the first two strophes, and which so well represent the tender but insistent calls of the serenader, are particularly effective when produced with the bell-like clarity of the highest-pitched voices (Ex.I).

Ex. I

The octave interval and downward fall to the dominant at "mein Mädchen," and similar triadic melodic passages at "sich regt" (both of course repeated at comparable places in the second strophe) suggest the same type of pure, almost vibratoless voice. They are also reminiscent of passages featuring the French Horn in Strauss' instrumental works.

Following the structure of the poem, the general outline of the song is A/A/B, with the three principal sections clearly delineated by long piano interludes, and shorter interludes setting off the rhymed couplets at the end of each sestet. The song's characteristic accompanying figure, basically a broken triad with the addition of a sixth, is first heard as a brief piano introduction (see Ex. I). It is an effective onomatopoeic analogue for the gentle rustling of the breeze through the leaves and/or the quiet murmuring of the brook. Although the idea of a musical analogue for one element of the text being used as a unifying device for the entire song is Schubertian in origin, the feeling evoked by Strauss' skillfully

arranged broken chords is Mendelssohnian in its fleet delicacy.
This light scherzando effect may very well have been inspired by
von Schack's reference to "Tritte der Elfen" (elves' steps) in the
central sestet.   When transferred to the lower registers of the
piano, as it is for the third sestet, the murmuring characteristic
figure becomes more intimate, reinforcing our assumption that the
two lovers are now close enough to one another to whisper rather
than call out their words of love (Ex. II).

Ex. II

The intimacy of the final strophe is further enhanced by the
slower pace of its melodic line.   While the accompaniment
maintains its tempo, the singer takes many more beats to state its
text; six measures suffice for the first two verses of the initial
strophe, while almost twice that number are necessary for the the
opening two lines of the last.   Having obtained his goal, our
protagonist is no longer in a hurry! The interlude preceding von
Schack's charming description of the titillated but embarrassed rose
features a melody previously heard in the vocal part. This little
piano solo is repeated after "Und die Rose," coyly delaying the
rest of the text. Strauss repeats the words "Hoch glühn," (hotly
glowing) thereby giving even greater significance to the image
while simultaneously allowing time for the vocal line to climb to
its highest point in the song. The postlude, delightfully charming
to the very end, fades away after reiterating most of the song's
significant melodic and harmonic material.

Chapter VII

HENRI DUPARC

PHIDYLE   poem by Leconte de Lisle

The second half of the nineteenth century in France saw a gradual movement away from the personal, the intimately sentimental, in all forms of literature. In reaction to the effusiveness of previous generations, a school of poets arose who stressed objectivity and erudition over spontaneity and idiosyncratic individuality. These post-Romantics placed the highest value on working their way to impeccable techniques, through which they hoped to achieve precision of line and beauty of form. Dubbed Parnassians because, in their love of Greek and Roman antiquity—and without undue modesty—they called their first collaborative collection of poetry *Le Parnasse contemporain* (1866), they agreed with their precursor and elder statesman, Théophile Gautier, (1811-1872) that a poem could rival a statue in its solidity and its plasticity. The poem was to convey a hard, physical presence equivalent to that of a work executed in marble or bronze. Gautier begins "l'Art," his much quoted manifesto, with the following words:

> Oui, l'oeuvre sort plus belle
> D'une forme au travail
>   Rebelle,
> Vers, marbre, onyx, émail.

> Yes, the most beautiful work comes
> From a type of labor which is
>   Resistant,
> Poetic lines, marble, onyx or enamel.

The last four stanzas of Gautier's poem further clarify his credo:

Tout passe—L'art robuste
Seul a l'éternité.
    Le buste
Survit à la cité.

Et la médaille austère
Que trouve un laboureur
    Sous terre
Révèle un empereur.

Les dieux eux-mêmes meurent.
Mais les vers souverains
    Demeurent
Plus forts que les airains.

Sculpte, lime, cisèle;
Que ton rêve flottant
    Se scelle
Dans le bloc résistant!

Everything passes—Robust art
Alone is eternal.
    The bust
Outlives the city.

And the austere medal
A laborer finds
    Underground
Reveals an emperor.

The gods themselves die.
But sovereign verses
    Remain
Stronger than brasses.

Sculpt, polish, chisel;
So that your vaporous dream
    May be sealed
In the recalcitrant block!

This poem first appeared in 1852 in a collection called *Emaux et Camées*, a slim volume of poetry by Gautier notable for its break with the Romantic aesthetic. "La vanité romantique, le faste des mots et des images, le moi n'ont plus rien à voir ici. Le poète est absent de son oeuvre" (Romantic vanity, the feast of words and images, the I are no longer to be seen here. The poet is absent from his work).[1]

In that same year, 1852, a collection called *Poèmes antiques* was published by the poet who was to become the leader of the Parnassian school, Leconte de Lisle (1820-1894). In a preface to this collection de Lisle set forth the program of the new anti-Romantic poetry: a turning away from "l'aveu public des angoisses du coeur" (the public avowal of agonies of the heart)[2] and a turning toward the attempt to reconcile art and science. To save this tightly controlled and impersonal poetry from cold insipidity, de Lisle filled his verses with exotica, relying on exquisitely crafted images of far off places, strange religions, unimaginable customs and unfamiliar plants and animals, to create a compelling atmosphere. This is undoubtedly the charm of "Phidylé."

PHIDYLE

L'herbe est molle au sommeil sous les frais peupliers,
Aux pentes des sources moussues,
Qui dans les prés en fleur germant par mille issues,
Se perdent sous les noirs halliers.

Repose, ô Phidylé! Midi sur les feuillages
Rayonne et t'invite au sommeil.
Par le trèfle et le thym, seules en plein soleil,
Chantent les abeilles volages;

Un chaud parfum circule au détour des sentiers,
La rouge fleur des blés s'incline,
Et les oiseaux, rasant de l'aile la colline,
Cherchent l'ombre des églantiers.

Mais, quand l'Astre, incliné sur sa courbe éclatante,
Verra ses ardeurs s'apaiser,

Que ton plus beau sourire et ton meilleur baiser
Me recompensent de l'attente!

PHIDYLE

The grass is soft for sleeping under the cool poplars,
At the slopes of the mossy springs,
Which, in the blossoming meadows sending out thousands of
  shoots,
Are lost in the black thickets.

Rest, Oh Phidylé! Noon on the leaves
Shines and invites you to sleep.
Amid the clover and the thyme, alone in the full sunlight,
The flying bees sing;

A warm perfume swirls around the curve of the paths,
The red flower of the wheat droops,
And the birds, scraping their wings against the hillside,
Look for the shadow of the sweetbriar.

But when the Star descending in its brilliant arc
Sees its ardors wane,
Let your most beautiful smile and your best kiss
Reward me for having waited!

The stanzas quoted above—those used by Duparc in his setting—are actually the first, second, third and last of this ten-stanza
"Poème antique." In those quatrains omitted by the composer, we
find several references to antiquity which make the work easily
identifiable as Parnassian: Diana, sitting in the depths of the
forest, polishing her deadly arrows; the lovely Erycine as she was
seen in the gardens of Sicily; and Nymphs at the threshold of their
ivy-covered grottos. All of these famous beauties, says the poet,
pale by comparison to Phidylé.

The most erotic lines in the poem are also found in the stanzas
not included by Duparc. We quote the sixth stanza as an example:

Laisse sur ton épaule et ses formes divines,
Comme un or fluide et léger,
Sous mon souffle amoureux courir et voltiger
L'épaisseur de tes tresses fines!

Allow on your shoulder and its divine shapes,
The thickness of your fine tresses,
Like light, liquid gold,
To run and ripple under my amorous breath!

Technically the poem cannot be faulted. Lines of twelve and
eight syllables alternate in its stanzas, and the complicated rhyme
scheme for the four quatrains included in the song is A B B A / C
A A C / A D D A / E A A E. The four sets of "A" end-sounds
are created by three different spellings—"...ers" in stanzas one and
three, "...eil" in the second strophe, and "...er" in the final
quatrain; their repetition and similar repetitions in the verses not
used by Duparc, coupled with the way in which they echo the
sound of the last syllable of the all-important word "Phidylé" give
the poem a unique, incantatory unity.

In the first stanza of "Phidylé" de Lisle paints a landscape in
which cool poplars and dark thickets on the mossy banks of a
stream provide a natural shelter whose soft grass beckons. He
then introduces a character with a Greek-sounding name, and joins
the mid-day sun in inviting her to rest, adding that only the bees
sing in the heat of noon. The air is heavy with perfume and the
birds seek relief from the sun in the shadow of the sweetbriar,
scraping their wings against the hillside in their quest for shade.
The speaker will wait for the sun ("L'Astre") to begin its descent
before coming to claim Phidylé's best smile and her best kiss as a
reward for his patience.

The poem moves from cool to warmth, from the impersonal to
the intimate, from the natural to the human. Although poplars
grow in France—as do moss, clover and thyme—and there are
occasionally days as hot and sultry as that described in the poem,
one imagines the setting to be some exotic tropical island, thereby
increasing its attraction. While the scenario would appear to be
heavily sensuous—a beautiful young woman resting all day in a
cool bower so as better to receive her lover at twilight—the verses

themselves are cool and detached. One has only to compare "Phidylé" to "Nahandove" (the first text in Maurice Ravel's *Chansons madécasses*), which is similar in setting and story outline, to sense the immediacy and intensity of the latter and the comparative remoteness of the former. It is just this sense of Parnassian distance that is overcome by Duparc's impassioned setting.

Henri Duparc (1848-1933) is a little-known, enigmatic figure. A student of César Franck, he began to study music relatively late in life and his penchant for extreme self-criticism led him to destroy almost everything he wrote, including some compositions that were highly valued by Franck and other composers of eminence. Virtually all that remains of his *oeuvre* are two orchestral works (a symphonic poem, *Lenore*, and *Aux Etoiles*, an orchestral nocturne), a vocal duet ("La Fuite"), and sixteen songs. In 1885 a strange mental collapse left him incapable of further work. He left Paris and went to Switzerland, where for the next forty-eight years he lived a reclusive and non-musical life. Despite the paucity of his output, Duparc holds a secure place in the history of French art song, for his sixteen surviving efforts in the genre are unforgettable and irreplaceable, each of them creating in its own way a sensuous yet ethereal world laden with mystery and yearning.

In the opening section of Duparc's setting of "Phidylé," repeated quarter-note chords, played slowly and calmly according to the composer's instructions, surround the quasi-recitativo vocal line with a breath-stopping stillness. (Ex. I)

Ex. I

Since there is an equivalent lack of motion in the melody, which hovers on or near the tonic note for the entire first quatrain and is to be sung softly and without nuance ("doux et sans nuances"), the poet's picture of a motionless landscape bathed in sleepy tranquillity, is well matched by the music.

A lovely enharmonic change introduces a new key for the words "Repose, ô Phidylé," which are treated in the song, albeit not in the poem, as a sort of refrain. Although in this second section there is more motion in the piano part, which now has a nice little countermelody in whole notes, the vocal line is even more languid than it was in the beginning: an entire four-beat measure each is given to the second and third syllables of "repose," and there is a six-beat pause for the singer after the significant phrase to set it apart from the rest of the line in which it occurs (Ex. II). Thus the music draws considerably more attention to the title-figure's exotic name and sultry nature than the poet can do within the technical framework of his text.

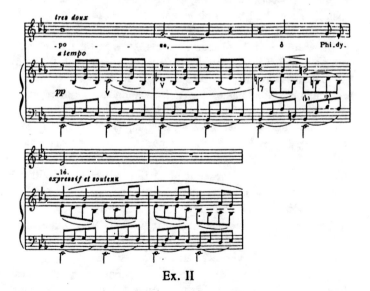

Ex. II

In the interlude after "Phidylé" the piano introduces a new melody which continues after the singer's reentry, eventually (under "t'invite au sommeil") resulting in a lovely duet in contrary

motion. Another key change, a concomitant move from eighth
-notes to triplets in the accompaniment and a generally quickened
pace, announce a new section in the music, although we are
mid-quatrain in the poem. Since the triplet figure immediately
yields to a sixteenth-note pattern, this section seems much livelier
than the first two. Despite this new feeling of agitation and
forward motion, to which frequent modulations add, the piano
interlude which has once again lengthened the intervals between
verses, stretches the poem in perceived as well as actual time.

Ever since Haydn's *Creation*—and perhaps even before it—
composers have been unable to resist a glorious modulation to a
full major chord whenever they set words portraying the coming
of light. Duparc does not disappoint, giving us a magnificent
chord progression to set off "en plein soleil." At the end of the
second stanza, while the singer is describing the sound of the bees,
the piano's impassioned melodic line soars above that of the
singer. The music continues to grow in power as the poet speaks
of the warm perfume that swirls around the paths, beginning its
metaphoric diminuendo and descent at the word "s'incline," the
"drooping" of the ripe wheat's red blossoms.

Between the third and fourth stanzas, separated from the rest of
the poem by long piano interludes, Duparc thrice repeats the words
"Repose, ô Phidylé," an addition to de Lisle's text. (In the
complete poem the name Phidylé is mentioned once more, in the
penultimate stanza: "Je charmerai les bois, ô blanche Phidylé, /
De ta louange familière; / Et les Nymphes, au seuil de leurs
grottes de lierre, / En pâliront, le coeur troublé." I shall charm
the woods, Oh white Phidylé, / With your familiar praise; / And
the Nymphs, at the threshold of their ivy grottos, / Will pale
because of it, their hearts disturbed.) The effectiveness of the
composer's use of verbal repetition not attempted by the poet
demonstrates that, since the music can be varied at each repetition,
this sort of device, which would seem tedious and contrived in a
literary text, works very well in a song.

Since the rhythm of the music has depended very little on de
Lisle's original format of three quatrains consisting of alternating
eight and twelve syllable verses, Duparc's liberty in no way
offends our ear. If it alters the meaning or impact of the poem, it

is only to make the listener focus more on the central figure and less on her surroundings, an effect which would probably not displease de Lisle. He himself had given the poem her name, a fact which is brought to the perceiver's attention less when listening to a song than when reading a poem. Yet, with the accompaniment's two gorgeous harmonic changes under "repose" in the first repeat, the vocal line's wonderful chromatic climb to the dominant note on "Phidylé" in the second, and the chromatically enriched pedal-point sustaining the hauntingly hushed tones of the third, this is one of the most beautiful segments of the song.

Whispering tremolos, which begin the next piano interlude, grow dynamically to a grand *forte* tonic chord. These few measures are more effective in the orchestral version Duparc subsequently made of the song—perhaps he was already thinking of the orchestration when he wrote them. The voice begins the final quatrain "with warmth" and *forte*, and the music rises to an enormous climax at the last line of text. The melody is triumphant in its diatonic march up to the tonic note, and the chords and tremolos in the accompaniment are heavy and noble. After the music has come to its passionate climax, a piano postlude gradually brings us to a calm, quiet conclusion.

Notes to Chapter VII

1. Théophile Gautier, *Pages choisies* (Classiques Larousse) p. 27.
2. Firmin Roz, *La Littérature française* (Allyn and Bacon, 1945) p. 262.

CHAPTER VIII

CLAUDE DEBUSSY

COLLOQUE SENTIMENTAL   poem by Paul Verlaine

For all the apparently iconoclastic elements it manifested when first published, the poetry of Paul Verlaine is now seen as part of the continuously developing tradition of French literature. Its sources of inspiration may be found in the texts of the poets who immediately preceded him—Victor Hugo, Théophile Gautier, Alphonse de Lamartine, Leconte de Lisle, Théodore de Banville and, above all, Charles Baudelaire. It may also be found in the paintings of the eighteenth-century artists Watteau, Boucher, Fragonard and Greuze. In turn, Verlaine became a father figure for the generation of poets who followed him. He was proclaimed on a par with Baudelaire as *chef d'école* by Symbolists and Decadents, and was appreciated and assimilated by such moderns as Apollinaire and Eluard.

Claude Debussy, whose works were at first regarded as so original as to be outside the mainstream of French music, has long since taken his rightful place of leadership within it. His harmonies are based as much on the ancient church modes and the parallel fifths and fourths common to all European music of the Middle Ages as they are on Javanese and other exotic sources, and the lightness and clarity typical of his style are redolent of the sound of eighteenth-century French clavichord music.

Neither Verlaine nor Debussy cared much for analysis of their works. The latter insisted that since he used chord combinations solely to please his ear and with no reference to rules of harmonization it would be useless to dissect his music for didactic purposes. Verlaine was equally opposed to a pedantic approach to poetry. "De la musique avant toute chose," (Music before everything else) he insisted in "L'Art poétique," the closest thing to a manifesto he ever wrote. "De la musique encore et toujours!" (Music again and always!)

By the music of poetry, two distinct characteristics are implied by Verlaine: the sensual, which depends on the sounds and rhythms of the words, and the abstract, i. e. that which is inherent in a text's imprecision, its disdain for discursive logic, its lack of specific referentiality. These are the very same factors that make music the perfect analogue for our deepest, most difficult to verbalize, emotions.

The notes of a musical composition—despite Debussy's claims to the contrary—most often have very specific meanings within the logical system of which they are a part, but are usually devoid of extramusical definition. Words, however, can never be totally free of referentiality no matter how idiosyncratically they are employed by the poet. Even nonsense syllables, as long as they can be pronounced within the normal speech patterns of the language, appear to borrow meaning from words they resemble, as Lewis Carroll and others have demonstrated. Nevertheless, all poetry save the overtly didactic seems to be an attempt to oppose normal referentiality, to surprise the reader into new insights through the use of ordinary words juxtaposed in extraordinary ways. The more successful is the poet at "driving a wedge between words and their meanings . . . and thereby inhibiting our flight from them to the things they point to,"[1] the more closely does the result resemble our definition of music, regardless of whether the language of the poetry is "musical" in its sound and rhythms.

To drive this wedge by his poetry's lightness, subtlety, vagueness, suggestiveness, and nuance was surely Verlaine's aim, and, in his opinion, the aim of all true poetry. To do so he preferred verses of odd numbers of feet rather than the twelve-syllable alexendrines so dear to French classicism. Furthermore, he vowed to eschew mordant wit, overly specific descriptions, strained or clever rhymes which call attention to themselves, and all other rhetorical devices.

Although he did not make such an avowal, one has the feeling that in his compositions Debussy was trying to drive a similar wedge between the musical sounds perceived at the moment and their referentiality to the known grammar of music. He certainly

made a point of avoiding the rhetoric of music with its precon-
ceived modulations and fillers.

Despite the fact that Verlaine claimed to be more influenced by
eighteenth-century art than by that of the Impressionists, his
collection *Fêtes Galantes* (six of whose poems, including "Colloque sentimental," Debussy chose to set to music) affords
numerous parallels to the paintings of Monet, Pissaro, Sisley and
Renoir. Like Verlaine, these visual artists wanted to suggest rather
than depict, to hint at subtle nuance, to allow the viewer to make
connections while they themselves avoided the precisely linear, the
pedantically symmetrical, the obtrusively clever academic tricks of
perspective, modeling and the like.

That Debussy subscribed to this Impressionist aesthetic is
obvious, and he is often labeled an Impressionist composer. By
and large avoiding the company of other musicians, he was on
most intimate terms with Manet, Mallarmé and other painters and
writers of the avant-garde. Over his long song-writing career,
from 1876 to 1915, he based five songs on poems by Baudelaire,
four on texts he wrote himself, four each on works by Mallarmé,
Paul Bourget and the seventeenth-century poet Tristan l'Hermite,
three each on works of Pierre Louÿs and François Villon, the great
fifteenth-century bard, and one or two on each of a handful of
diverse French poets. What greater proof of his affinity for
Verlaine could there be than the fact that eighteen of Debussy's
songs are settings for poems by that particular lyric artist?

"Colloque sentimental" is the last of twenty-two poems in a
collection by Verlaine called *Fêtes galantes*, and the last of a group
of three songs called *Fêtes galantes II* by Debussy. (Debussy's
Fêtes galantes I consists of settings of three poems from the
beginning of Verlaine's collection.) This "Sentimental dialogue,"
as it is called in a title steeped in irony, can stand alone either as
a poem or as a song, but its stark despair and its atmosphere of
death and disillusion are all the more potent in its intended
positions within the poetry collection and within the vocal group.

All of Verlaine's *Fêtes galantes* is based on material which
allowed the poet to map out his own personal poetic terrain, a
magical arena in which outer manifestations of the natural world
are mystically fused with the soul of man. The opening text,
"Clair de lune," which was the inspiration for two Debussy songs

as well as one of the composer's best known piano pieces, begins

> Votre âme est un paysage choisi
> Que vont charmants masques et bergamasques,
> Jouant du luth et dansant, et quasi
> Tristes sous leurs déguisements fantasques!

> Your soul is a chosen landscape
> Where spell-binding masqueraders and dancers,
> Play the lute and dance,
> And are almost sad under their fantastic disguises!

The very first line of the lyric alerts the reader that all that is to follow, not only in this poem but in the collection as a whole, will be a metaphor for the soul, not only the soul of the poet, but your soul, dear reader, "mon semblable, mon frère" (my counterpart, my brother) as Baudelaire might have said. But only a reader with a soul sensitive and flexible enough to empathize with that of Verlaine will be able to follow the poet's journey through this veiled landscape, where everyone is disguised, where descriptions of commonplace emotions such as sadness are undermined by disturbing qualifiers like "almost," where references to antique instruments, archaic turns of phrase ("que vont" instead of où vont) and obscure allusions (a bergamasque is both someone from the area once known by that name and a dance characteristic of it) erode the reader's sense of time and place.

Having established the metaphoric role of this singular landscape, Verlaine goes on to people it with masked dancers in fantastic disguises whose minor-mode music sings of a happiness too fragile to be trusted. Inanimate objects reflect the actors' moods, for the moonlight is sad as well as beautiful and the fountains sob with ecstasy.

Despite the "almost sad" in the first quatrain of "Clair de lune," the opening few texts of *Fêtes galantes* are joyous and gay, full of sparkling, iridescent, fantasy-filled evocations of the world of the privileged in pre-Revolutionary eighteenth-century France as depicted by Watteau, Boucher, Fragonard and Greuze. There is a general movement from joy to despondency, from ecstasy to despair, in the collection as a whole as well as in some of the

individual songs ("En sourdine," for example). This movement
culminates in the bleak *tête-à-tête* called "Colloque sentimental."

COLLOQUE SENTIMENTAL

Dans le vieux parc solitaire et glacé
Deux formes ont tout à l'heure passé.

Leurs yeux sont morts et leurs lèvres sont molles,
Et l'on entend à peine leurs paroles.

Dans le vieux parc solitaire et glacé
Deux spectres ont évoqué le passé.

—Te souvient-il de notre extase ancienne?
—Pourquoi voulez-vous donc qu'il m'en souvienne?

—Ton coeur bât-il toujours à mon seul nom?
Toujours vois-tu mon âme en rêve?—Non.

—Ah! les beaux jours de bonheur indicible
Où nous joignions nos bouches!—C'est possible.

—Qu'il était bleu, le ciel, et grand, l'espoir!
—L'esprit a fui, vaincu, vers le ciel noir.

Tels ils marchaient dans les avoines folles,
Et la nuit seule entendit leurs paroles.

SENTIMENTAL DIALOGUE

In the old deserted and frozen park
Two forms just passed by.

Their eyes are dead and their lips are slack,
And one scarcely hears their words.

In the old deserted and frozen park
Two specters evoked the past.

—Do you remember our old ecstasy?
—Why then do you want me to remember it?

—Does your heart still beat at the mention of my name?
Do you still see my soul in your dreams? — No.

—Ah the beautiful days of unspeakable happiness
When our lips were joined!—It's possible.

—How blue was the sky, and how great was hope!
—The spirit has fled, vanquished, toward the black sky.

So they walked in the wild wheat,
And only the night heard their words.

It seems safe to say that, despite the touches of irony, hints of
disillusionment and gentle evocations of melancholy found in other
poems of *Fêtes galantes*, the reader is not really prepared for the
mordant bitterness, the naked despair of this, its closing piece.
This bleak exchange between two pale wraiths, overheard in the
frigid, deserted park by a disembodied narrator whose own
existence is denied in the poem's last line (And only the night
heard their words), refuses the one solace expected by all
lovers—memory of their moments of bliss. Actually one of the
pair does remember—we are not told which one—but the denials
of the other negate these memories with chilling persistence.

The poem, probably inspired by Théophile Gautier's "Le banc
de pierre" ("Au fond d'un parc, dans une ombre indécise / Il est
un banc solitaire et moussu...Ce banc désert regrette le passé . .
."), is remarkably balanced, with three rhymed couplets which set
the scene and one couplet which serves as a postlude surrounding
the four couplets of the actual dialogue. The first and third pairs
of lines are very similar, both ending in "glacé"/"passé"; the
differences between them are the substitution of "spectres" for
"formes"—a change which makes the subjects of the poem even
more pitifully ghostlike than they first appeared—and the replace-
ment of the phrase "ont tout à l'heure passé" with "ont évoqué le
passé," which moves the action along. There are different end

sounds for each of the couplets of the "colloque," but the introductory and summarizing pairs of lines have but two end-sounds; this repetition of rhymes as well as that of the word "paroles" in the last line link the opening couplets to one another and to the end.

The dialogue is not divided evenly between the two speakers, for the lover who cannot or will not remember is much more terse than the partner provoking the exchange. His or her two briefest answers, "non" and "C'est possible," are the most chilling of the four, for they seem to resist the sharing that even this despondent dialogue implies. To further underscore the difference between the two characters, the more laconic of them uses the distancing "vous," the other the intimate "tu." The language and structure of the poem reflect the frozen quality of the setting and the sentiment, for the lines are kept within a rigid ten-foot norm with not a single *enjambement* to vary the pace. There is decidedly more movement in the language of the phrases of the lover who remembers than in the partner's responses, however, and this repeated change in tempo, coupled with Verlaine's supple manipulation of cesura, prevents the poem from seeming stolid.

The piano introduction to Debussy's setting of "Colloque sentimental" consists of two melodies, both based on the whole-tone scale. Like the lovers in the text, the two melodies seem to be at cross purposes. The first meanders aimlessly, sometimes in duple, sometimes in triplet eighth-notes, while the second marches in steady duple eighths or quarters in a definite downward direction (Ex. I).

Ex. I

The chill and lonely mood immediately established by the emptiness of the single notes in the first bar is sustained by the initial unaccompanied vocal line (Ex. II) and the repeated note on which nine of the ten syllables of the second line are intoned does nothing to lighten the gloom. The four remaining lines of introductory narrative are confined to few changes of pitch while the piano repeats its introductory melody in accompaniment.

Ex. II

At the word "spectres" a C natural is heard in the piano part; this becomes the significant note for the central section of the song. It is present in every measure of the dialogue and as such provides a metaphor for the sometimes steady, sometimes halting steps the two specters take as they talk (Ex. III).

Ex. III

A melancholy, expressive chord, played as though from afar, begins the actual dialogue section. After a two-bar piano solo the first voice enters with a reasonably flowing melodic line whose sixteenth-notes give considerable movement to the words. When the second voice responds the tempo is held back and the intervals are more restricted. The tempo moves ahead again for the next two questions asked by the first voice, whose increased agitation can be assumed from the *crescendo* and rising melodic line given

to "toujours à mon seul nom?" The climactic high note on "nom"
is followed by an octave drop and a semi-recitative for the next
line of text. The one-syllable answer "Non" is sung on a low E,
perhaps an indication, as most would suspect, that the recalcitrant
partner is the male.

The music becomes faster and louder to indicate mounting
excitement and agitation on the first speaker's part, reaching a
peak for singer and pianist at the extended word "indicible." This
climactic moment is followed by the quiet hush of ecstasy as the
first voice relives the erotic past, but an increase in tempo
deliberately interrupts the mood as the second voice answers
impatiently, "C'est possible." The music is quiet and subdued for
the final exchange, reaching its lowest point on the pessimistic
"noir" of the last response. The reiterated C natural, representa-
tive of the couple's pacing, ceases as the epilogue begins. Here
the accompaniment barely supports the *quasi-recitativo* melody; it
then stops altogether while the voice solemnly intones "Et la nuit
seule." Different versions of a flute-like figure reminiscent of a
bird-call had been heard in the piano part during the dialogue
section; this figure returns at the last line of text (Ex. IV).

Ex. IV

At this point the tonal center, C sharp minor, begins to assert
itself as though in preparation for the fade-out ending, which

consists of the little flute figure, played ever more quietly and slowly. This onomatopoeic representation of the lone bird—most probably a nightingale—is Debussy's musical version of Verlaine's invocation of nature as the only possible witness to man's despair.

HARMONIE DU SOR   Charles Baudelaire

In 1857 two major literary events occurred in Paris: the much awaited publication of Gustave Flaubert's novel *Madame Bovary* and the somewhat startling appearance of Charles Baudelaire's collection of poems, *Les Fleurs du mal*. These two works, which presaged the cultural era many consider the most important in France since the age of Classicism in the seventeenth-century court of Louis XIV—that of the Symbolist poets and Impressionist painters and composers—share more than a birthdate, for both resulted in lawsuits in which their authors were charged with promoting public immorality. *Madame Bovary* and its author were exonerated, but six of Baudelaire's poems, henceforth referred to as "Les Pièces condamnées" and not published legally in France until 1949, were found obscene and expunged from the collection; Baudelaire was himself fined and reprimanded.

Nothing helps the sale of a book more than a well-publicized scandal, especially when the cause of the uproar is a charge of salaciousness, and the two works in question were immediately widely read and discussed. In the case of these masterpieces, however, titillation was only a temporary boost. The power of Flaubert's prose and Baudelaire's poetry would have made its impact quite apart from the scandal surrounding their publication.

With their rejection of the Hugoesque ideal of Art at the service of the social order; with their shared goal of scientific precision—"le mot juste"—to express the most ephemeral poetic experiences; with their determination to give objective, detached representations of the most intimate personal thoughts and feelings no matter how unspontaneous the finished works might be, the authors of *Madame Bovary* and *Les Fleurs du mal* brought the age of Romanticism to an end in France.

Flaubert's great novel is generally considered the seminal work for the prose writers who followed him. Despite his disdain for the Realist and Naturalist schools which claimed to base their theories on *Madame Bovary* and Flaubert's later work, *L'Education sentimentale*, and his reluctance to be included under their rubrics, Flaubert's influence is clearly discernible in the fiction of such masters as Realist-Naturalists Jules and Edmond Goncourt and Emile Zola. Baudelaire, on the other hand, seems more at ease under the banner of Symbolism, the school which took its lead from his poetry. It shared with the author of *Les Fleurs du mal* one of his most important concepts, that of the "correspondence" of all things.

CORRESPONDANCES

La Nature est un temple où de vivants piliers
Laissent parfois sortir de confuses paroles;
L'homme y passe à travers des forêts de symboles
Qui l'observent avec des regards familiers.

Comme de longs échos qui de loin se confondent
Dans une ténébreuse et profonde unité,
Vaste comme la nuit et comme la clarté,
Les parfums, les couleurs et les sons se répondent.

Il est des parfums frais comme des chairs d'enfants,
Doux comme les hautbois, verts comme les prairies,
—Et d'autres, corrompus, riches et triomphants,

Ayant l'expression des choses infinies,
Comme l'ambre, le musc, le benjoin et l'encens,
Qui chantent les transports de l'esprit et des sens.

Nature is a temple from which living columns
Sometimes allow confused words to emanate;
Man passes across these forests of symbols
Which observe him with familiar glances.

Like long echoes which mingle from afar
In a shadowy and profound unity,
Vast as the night and daylight,
Scents, colors and sounds are in harmony with one
    another.

There are perfumes as fresh as the flesh of children,
As soft as oboes, as green as prairies,
—And others, corrupt, rich and triumphant,

Having the expression of infinite things,
Like amber, musk, aromatic resin and incense,
Which sing of the raptures of the spirit and the senses.

The poem cited above, the fourth text in *Les Fleurs du mal*,
served as a sort of manifesto for the Symbolists who followed
Baudelaire.   Many other of his elegantly expressed but often
bitterly mordant ideas became catchwords for the younger
generation of writers. His opening address "Au lecteur," to the
reader, for example, begins

La sottise, l'erreur, le péché, la lésine,
Occupent nos esprits et travaillent nos corps,
Et nous alimentons nos aimables remords,
Comme les mendiants nourrissent leur vermine.

Stupidity, error, sin, stinginess,
Occupy our spirits and work on our bodies,
And we nourish our amiable remorse,
As beggars feed their lice.

After citing horror after horror, evil after evil, the poem
concludes

Il en est un plus laid, plus méchant, plus immonde!
Quoiqu'il ne pousse ni grands gestes ni grands cris,
Il ferait volontiers de la terre un débris
Et dans un bâillement avalerait le monde;

C'est l'Ennui!—l'oeil chargé d'un pleur involontaire,
Il rêve d'échafauds en fumant son houka.
Tu le connais, lecteur, ce monstre délicat,
—Hypocrite lecteur,—mon semblable,—mon frère!

There is one uglier, more wicked, more foul!
Although he makes no grand gestures, utters no great
  cries,
He would willingly make debris of the earth
And with a yawn would swallow the world;

He is Ennui!—his eye heavy with an unwilled tear,
He dreams of scaffolds while smoking his hooka.
You know him, reader, this delicate monster,
—Hypocritical reader,—my fellowman—my brother!

In "L'Albatros," the second poem in the collection, Baudelaire describes the poet in unforgettable terms:

Le Poète est semblable au prince des nuées
Qui hante la tempête et se rit de l'archer;
Exilé sur le sol au milier des huées,
Ses ailes de géant l'empêchent de marcher.

The Poet is like the prince of storm clouds
Who haunts the storm and laughs at the bowman;
Exiled on the ground in the midst of derision,
His giant-size wings prevent him from walking.

An "obscure enemy" gnaws away at the poet's heart while Time eats up his life ("L'Ennemi"); a strange "guignon" or jinx dogs his steps. His idea of beauty, "un rêve de pierre" (a dream made of stone) which floats in the blue "comme un sphinx incompris," (like an uncomprehended sphinx) is close to that of the Parnassians, except that Baudelaire's beauty is one on whose breast "chacun s'est meurtri tour à tour" (everyone is murdered in turn). "La Beauté" herself speaks:

J'unis un cœur de neige à la blancheur des cygnes;
Je hais le mouvement qui déplace les lignes,
Et jamais je ne pleure et jamais je ne ris.

I join a heart of snow with the whiteness of swans;
I hate the movement which disturbs the lines,
And I never laugh and I never cry.

Baudelaire loves the exotic perfumes, the wildly curling hair, the languid airs and strange indifference of creole women. In one poem, "Une Charogne," one of the six "Pièces condamnées," he imagines his loved one as a corpse, "Les jambes en l'air, comme une femme lubrique, / Brûlante et suant les poisons," (Legs in the air, like a lubricious woman / Burning and sweating poisons); in another "L'Aube spirituelle," he sees her as the "chère Déesse, Etre lucide et pur," (dear Goddess, lucid and pure being) whose memory, "plus clair, plus rose, plus charmant," (brighter, pinker, more charming) rises from "les débris fumeux des stupides orgies" (the smoldering debris of stupid orgies).

Everywhere in the works of Baudelaire one finds contradictions: he is torn between hope and ennui, filled at the same time with the spleen that comes from having "plus de souvenirs que si j'avais mille ans" (more memories than if I were a thousand years old: "Spleen") and with a tranquil joy in the beauty of the "sons et parfums [qui] tournent dans l'air du soir" (the sounds and perfumes [which] turn in the evening air: "L'Harmonie du soir"); he sees himself as "un faux accord / Dans la divine symphonie," (a discord in the divine symphony), at once "la plaie et le couteau . . . le soufflet et la joue...les membres et la roue...la victime et le bourreau" (the wound and the knife...the slap and the cheek...the limbs and the rack . . . the victim and the executioner: "L'Héautontimorouménos"). His very awareness of his debauchery makes him long for purity—Satan himself has the power to seduce only because he carries within him memories of the Angel.[2]

The duality so characteristic of Baudelaire's themes is carried into his poetic technique, for his most disorderly, melodramatic and subjective thoughts, his most opaque, provocative and self-contradictory images, are more often than not expressed in alexandrines as solid and sonorous as those of Racine.[3] That this may present a problem for the post-Romantic composer did not deter Debussy from setting five of Baudelaire's poems to music—"Le Balcon," "Le Jet d'eau," "Recueillement," "La Mort des amants," and "Harmonie du soir." It is on this last named poem that we shall focus our discussion.

HARMONIE DU SOIR

Voici venir le temps où vibrant sur sa tige
Chaque fleur s'évapore ainsi qu'un encensoir;
Les sons et les parfums tournent dans l'air du soir;
Valse mélancolique et langoureux vertige!

Chaque fleur s'évapore ainsi qu'un encensoir;
Le violon frémit comme un coeur qu'on afflige;
Valse mélancolique et langoureux vertige!
Le ciel est triste et beau comme un grand reposoir.

Le violon frémit comme un coeur qu'on afflige;
Un coeur tendre qui hait le néant vaste et noir!
Le ciel est triste et beau comme un grand reposoir.
Le soleil s'est noyé dans son sang qui se fige.

Un coeur tendre qui hait le néant vaste et noir,
Du passé lumineux recueille tout vestige!
Le soleil s'est noyé dans son sang qui se fige . . .
Ton souvenir en moi luit comme un ostensoir!

HARMONY OF THE EVENING

Now comes the time when trembling on its stem
Each flower gives off scent like a censer;
Sounds and scents turn in the evening air;
Melancholy waltz and langorous vertigo!

Each flower gives off scent like a censer;
The violin shudders like a heart one afflicts;
Melancholy waltz and languorous vertigo!
The sky is sad and beautiful like a great altar.

The violin shudders like a heart one afflicts;
A tender heart that hates the vast, black void!
The sky is sad and beautiful like a great altar.
The sun has drowned itself in its congealing blood.

A tender heart that hates the vast, black void,
From the luminous past gathers all remains!
The sun has drowned itself in its congealing blood. . .
Your memory shines within me like a shrine!

All through the first half of the nineteenth century, Romantic
French poets had fought against the tyranny of the Classical
alexandrine, with its inflexible twelve syllable length and its
formulaic pause after the sixth syllable. Now, through the efforts
of Lamartine, Alfred de Musset, and above all Victor Hugo, that
the battle had been won, Baudelaire elects to write a beautifully
limpid, exquisitely flowing poem in the strictest Racinian manner.
With the exception of the line "Un coeur tendre, qui hait le néant
vaste et noir," where the natural break comes after the fourth
syllable, every verse in "Harmonie du soir" is so constructed by
the poet that even without punctuation the reader will pause
midway through, and no thought is carried by an "enjambement"
from one line to the next.

Borrowing a device from the troubadours of the Middle Ages,
Baudelaire uses each line of verse twice, the second and fourth
lines of each stanza serving as the first and third lines of the next.
The opening and closing lines of the poem alone go unrepeated.
This complex scheme gives the poet only two end sounds for the
entire poem: "oir" and "ige." The resulting rhyme scheme is A B
B A / B A A B / A B B A / B A A B.

Baudelaire's imagery is derived partly from nature—flowers
trembling on their stems, the setting sun—and partly from the
Catholic Church service—the incense burner, the grand altar, the
holy shrine. Often these images are inextricably intertwined, for
the scent of the flowers is like that of the incense burner and the
sky is as beautiful as a grand altar. Nature and human emotions
are just as inseparable, for the sky is sad and the sun drowns itself
in its own congealing blood. Sounds like that of the violin, so

similar to that of a wounded heart, mix with scents, creating the self-contradictory images of melancholy waltzes and languorous vertigos. The almost motionlesss, twilight landscape, shimmering with sounds and scents, is identified by juxtaposition with the soul of the poet, as "ton souvenir" glows in him like a shrine.

Debussy was obviously much smitten with this text, not only setting it to music in its entirety, but also using one of its verses, "Les sons et les parfums tournent dans l'air du soir," as the title of one of his most atmospheric piano *Préludes*. Although the song setting is basically in the key of B major, Debussy has the piano begin with a C sharp minor triad, which is immediately followed by a characteristic figure consisting of triplet sixteenth notes—an apt musical representation of things "turning in the air" (Ex. I). Of the first ten notes of the melody, all but the first are at whole-tone intervals, a pattern which is more or less this composer's trademark.

Ex. I.

From the very first line, one can see that Debussy is not interested in strict adherence to Baudelaire's carefully worked-out *césures* (breaks after the sixth syllable), for the rhythmic setting of "Voici venir le temps" creates a pause after the second syllable, exemplifying the maxim that when there is a conflict between the meter of a poem and the rhythm of its setting, the music is always more powerful than the text. Nevertheless Baudelaire's meter is honored by Debussy in more than half the sixteen lines of the poem—in the twice-heard "Le violon frémit," "Le ciel est triste et beau," "Un coeur tendre," (here the natural pause in the music is after the fourth syllable, as it is in the poem), "Le soleil s'est noyé" and "Du passé lumineux," and the unrepeated "Ton souvenir en moi."

Debussy's choice of rhythm has an interesting effect on the poem's first line: it emphasizes the inner rhyme of "temps" and "vibrant," while making the alliteration of "Voici" and "venir" less prominent. Similarly, the phrase "Les sons et les parfums tournent dans l'air du soir" has considerable swirling motion with a pause, as placed by Debussy, after "sons," for this rhythmic division allows the uninterrupted flow of the remaining ten syllables. The more ordinary *césure* after the sixth syllable, which was probably intended by Baudelaire, breaks the motion into two briefer segments. The deliberate rhythmic monotony of the repeated triplet eighth-notes Debussy writes in the vocal part for "Valse mélancolique et langoureux vertige" robs the line of any dance-like quality it might have had, laying stress on the melancholy and languid aspects of Baudelaire's imagery; but the agitated piano accompaniment contradicts the limited motion in the melody, its busy arpeggios suggesting the giddy dizziness of vertigo. Thus Debussy retains the contradictions inherent in Baudelaire's text.

Ex. II

For the much-quoted line "Les sons et les parfums" Debussy chooses a C sharp minor-B major-A major sequence reminiscent of the harmonies he had used in the opening bars. The last note of this melodic phrase, the half-step up to G natural on "soir", is the most beautiful, and its harmonization (a G suspension over an A chord) is equally moving.

Once again, in the fourth line of text, it is the note on which the last syllable of a phrase is sung (the D sharp of "encensoir") that captures the listener's attention, for, spelled E flat in the accompaniment, it permits the introduction of a most effective C minor chord. (Ex. II.)

At this point the complex scheme of the poem begins to make itself evident in both text and music. Debussy uses Baudelaire's pattern to shape his setting, repeating musical material when the text is reiterated, but varying the keys and the endings so that free harmonic flow can be maintained. When "Le violon frémit comme un coeur qu'on afflige" is repeated, for example, the vocal line rises at the end of the phrase instead of falling as it had the first time those words were heard. This permits Debussy to introduce new musical material for the first statement of "Un coeur tendre."

The music is at its simplest for the tranquil words "Le ciel est triste et beau." The melody is basically a sequentially stated D major seventh and the harmony a varicolored G resolving to C major for the first statement, with the whole pattern transposed down a whole step when the line is repeated.

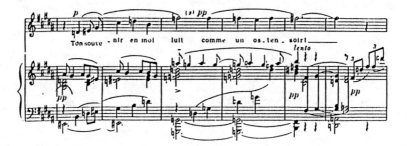

Ex. III

Debussy uses a whole-tone pattern for both statements of the chilling words "Le soleil s'est noyé dans son sang qui se fige," creating a serenity seemingly unaffected by the poet's disquieting imagery until the melancholy drop at the end of the phrase. Throughout the setting, in an appropriate reflection of Baudelaire's allusions to Catholic pageantry (a combination of the sensuous and the religious was part but by no means all of what Victor Hugo called the "nouveau frisson"—the new shudder—Baudelaire contributed to French poetry) Debussy's music evokes a mood of reverence. The high F natural on which the significant word "luit" (shines or glows) is sung seems to be climactic, coming as it does from the B natural an augmented fourth below (the forbidden devil's interval of medieval lore), but its yielding to an F sharp on the last syllable is the real climax of the piece, and it is indeed a moment of supre: ; beauty (Ex. III.)

CHANSONS DE BILITIS   texts by Pierre Louÿs

The three "Chansons de Bilitis," the subject of the ensuing discussion, are the result of a literary hoax. Pierre Louÿs, the actual author of the texts, claimed to have discovered and translated these poems which, according to him, were written by an unknown Greek poetess. Like original forgeries in painting, as opposed to copies of existing works, the merits of hybrids such as the "Chansons de Bilitis" are highly debatable; in the case of Louÿs' little game, the musical response they evoked in Debussy has earned them a permanent place in the legitimate canon.

Creative hoaxes, be they scientific, artistic or literary, are usually fun. Assuming that no harm is done—no fortunes lost, no bogus cures substituted for effective medication, no deserving reputations sullied—there is a certain malicious pleasure for the layperson in seeing the experts baffled, the cognoscenti befuddled. The general acceptance of Louÿs' claims for his "Chansons" may be taken as a measure of the familiarity, or lack thereof, of the nineteenth-century French literati of the authentic Greek idyll, the genre to which Louÿs claimed the works of his imaginary author belonged.

The earliest idylls known to literary criticism are those of Theocritus, who lived in the third century before Christ. Louÿs places his Bilitis lyrics some three hundred years before those of this acknowledged founder of the Hellenistic pastoral tradition. He states in his introduction to the published *Chansons de Bilitis* that his poetess was born at the beginning of the sixth century B. C. in a village on the banks of the Mélas. The daughter of a Greek father and a Phoenician mother, Louÿs continues in his detailed biography of the non-existent writer, the young Bilitis led a pastoral life. After some unfortunate episodes, including the birth of an illegitimate child, Bilitis moved to the island of Lesbos where, "les maris occupés par le vin et les danseuses, les femmes devaient fatalement se rapprocher et trouver entre elles la consolation de leur solitude" (their husbands occuped with wine and dancing girls, the women had, fatally, to become close to one another and find among themselves consolation for their solitude).

In Lesbos Bilitis met Sapho (sic) who, although no longer young, was still beautiful. In admiration of the older woman and in accordance with the customs of the island whose name has become synonymous with female homosexuality, Bilitis took a beautiful young woman as her lover. Her descriptions of this beloved Mytilène are full of tenderness and praise. Bilitis' life included interludes as a courtesan; her experiences, hetero- as well as homosexual, were varied, providing the material for her exotic poetry.

Louÿs claims to have gotten the above-stated information from the work of a German scholar who had discovered Bilitis' tomb, "a roomy cave covered with limestone slabs on which were etched in primitive capital letters all the songs you will read here." In 1900 the venerable and reliable Parisian firm of Charpentier et Pasquelle published *Les Chansons de Bilitis* as translations from the Greek by Pierre Louÿs. The book's preface consisted of the biographical data here summarized as well as Louÿs' account of the archeological discovery through which the life and work of Bilitis supposedly became known to him. Before the "translation" of the first poem are two lines, in Greek, from Theocritus' Idyll XX:

> Pleasant my piping, melodious, whether I play on the
> Pan-pipes
> Or on the babbling flute, or a reed, or the transverse
> recorder.

Louÿs, claiming that he could not do justice to the Greek originals
in French verse, offered his "translations" in prose.

LA FLÛTE DE PAN

Pour le jour des Hyacinthes,
Il m'a donné une syrinx faite
De roseaux bien taillés,
Unis avec la blanche cire
Qui est douce à mes lèvres comme le miel.
Il m'apprend à jouer, assise sur ses genoux;
Mais je suis un peu tremblante.
Il en joue après moi, si doucement
Que je l'entends à peine.
Nous n'avons rien à nous dire,
Tant nous sommes près l'un de l'autre;
Mais nos chansons veulent se répondre,
Et tour à tour nos bouches
S'unissent sur la flûte.
Il est tard;
Voici le chant des grenouilles vertes
Qui commence avec la nuit.
Ma mère ne croira jamais
Que je suis restée si longtemps
A chercher ma ceinture perdue.

PAN'S FLUTE

For the day of Hyacinthus
He gave me a syrinx made
Of well-trimmed reeds,
Held together with white wax
Which is as sweet as honey to my lips.
He teaches me to play, seated on his knees;
But I tremble a little.
He plays after me, so softly
That I scarcely hear him.
We have nothing to say to one another,
So close we are to one another;

But our songs want to be in harmony,
And little by little our mouths
Join on the flute.
It is late;
Now the song of the green frogs
Begins with nightfall.
My mother will never believe
That I stayed here so long
Looking for my lost sash.

Bilitis was supposedly still a young girl when she wrote
Bucolique de Pamphylle, the group of poems from which the three
"Chansons de Bilitis" are taken, and in "La Flûte de Pan," the first
of these lyrics to be set by Debussy, Louÿs captures very well the
demure, shy, apprehensive candor of an inexperienced adolescent
who is feeling for the first time the erotic tinglings of physical
attraction. The sentence structure in Louÿs' French "translation"
is simple, innocent, guileless. Even the expression of the fib the
girl will offer to her mother is so artless as to be free of the stigma
of subterfuge.

Ex. I

Debussy's setting of Louÿs' charming prose-poem is elegant, sensitive, and absolutely characteristic of its composer. The not-quite whole-tone scale harmonized by a major-seventh chord (B, D#, F#, A#) in the opening measure, the change from 4/4 to 3/4 meter in the first two bars, the unprepared movement from a C sharp major to a B major chord at the end of the second measure, the use of both regular and triplet eighth-notes in the singer's first phrase—these are all Debussy trademarks, none the less beautiful, of course, for being part of his standard vocabulary, and, although identifiable as Impressionistic, peculiarly evocative of a vague antiquity. (Ex. I)

The scale figure with which the song opens is an obvious reference to the flute, an instrument Debussy loved, as his setting of Mallarmé's *Prélude à l'après-midi d'un faune* will attest. The three-note pattern first heard at "unis avec la blanche cire," repeated three times by the voice and then taken up by the accompaniment for the next five measures, might be the novice flutist practicing her first lesson (Ex. II).

Ex. II

Following the descriptive mode already established in the setting, Debussy has the voice sink tremulously for the words "je

suis un peu tremblante" and again for "j'entends à peine." The
melodic line becomes highly chromatic under "mais nos chansons
veulent se répondre," and the equally chromatic rise under "nos
bouches s'unissent sur la flûte" gives a sense of climactic arrival
despite the *ritard* and *pp* dynamics.

As soon as Bilitis has told us of her lips uniting on the flute with
those of her master, the accompaniment paints a joyous picture of
two flutes playing at once, one darting over and under the other.
The voice interrupts this idyll with the warning words "Il est tard,"
gravely intoned on one pitch. The two flutes—or are they two
reeds of a double-aulos?—cannot ignore the admonition. After two
measures of subdued play they yield to light chords and a grace-
note figure that may represent the sound of the frogs the girl now
brings to our attention. The last lines of the song are delivered in
a quasi-recitative style, "almost without voice" as the composer
instructs the singer, and at an increased pace, for she really must
hurry. The postlude, similar to the introduction, is heard as
though from far away, the master still playing while the girl speeds
home. The final antique-sounding chords remind us that this all
happened long, long ago.

LA CHEVELURE

Il m'a dit: "Cette nuit, j'ai rêvé.
J'avais ta chevelure autour de mon cou.
J'avais tes cheveux comme un collier noir
Autour de ma nuque et sur ma poitrine.
Je les caressais, et c'étaient les miens;
Et nous étions liés pour toujours ainsi,
Par la même chevelure, la bouche sur la bouche,
Ainsi que deux lauriers n'ont souvent qu'un racine.
Et peu à peu il m'a semblé,
Tant nos membres étaient confondus,
Que je devenais toi-même,
Ou que tu entrais en moi comme mon songe."
Quand il eut achevé,
Il mit doucement ses mains sur mes épaules,
Et il me regarda d'un regard si tendre
Que je baissai les yeux avec un frisson.

THE HAIR

He said to me: "Last night I had a dream.
I had your hair around my neck.
I had your tresses like a black collar
Around my neck and on my breast.
I caressed them, and they were mine;
And we were joined for all time thus,
By the same hair, mouth upon mouth,
Just as two laurel trees often have but one root.
And little by little it seemed to me,
Our limbs were so intertwined,
That I became you,
Or that you entered into me like my dream."
When he had finished,
He gently put his hands on my shoulders,
And he looked at me with a glance so tender
That I lowered my eyes with a shiver.

This passionate and tender prose-poem is far more than an expression of purely physical love. The dream-image the young man describes—two beings so entwined as to seem two laurels with but one root—implies spiritual as well as erotic union. The lovers in the dream are at the same time two separate beings and one unique soul; she enters him as his own thoughts do and he becomes her very self. In the tradition of Baudelaire and the English pre-Raphaëlites, the speaker is obsessed with his beloved's hair; it surrounds him, holding him captive, and as he caresses her luxuriant tresses they seem to be his own. The last word of the text, "frisson," leaves the reader as well as the speaker shaken by the intensity of the passion it evokes.

In contrast to "La Flûte de Pan," "La Chevelure" contains no allusions to Greek society—no "syrinx made of well-trimmed reeds," no "day of Hyacinthus," no "white wax sweet as honey" to establish authentic-sounding connections to antiquity. The man and woman in this second "Chanson" could be a couple from any place and any time. To this reader they seem completely contemporary.

Ex. I

Debussy's setting begins quietly and slowly, with the introductory chords floating from augmented to major and back again in a gently-rocking 6/4 meter (Ex. I.)   These harmonies create a mysterious aura, so that when the voice enters somberly with "Il m'a dit," we are prepared to hear an extraordinary tale.

The voice pauses as the piano, at a slightly quickened pace, introduces a melodic line surrounded by B flat-seven chords. The singer then joins the piano's melody for her next phrase (the song must be sung by a woman to make any sense of the text); this phrase is still somewhat introductory in nature ("Cette nuit j'ai rêvé").   As the story begins to unfold, the music reflects the growing intensity and excitement of the speaker, small crescendi indicating interim climactic points along the way. The vocal line is often quasi-recitative, and primarily based on whole-tone intervals ("Je les caressais, et c'étaient les miens, et nous étions liés pour toujours ainsi" is sung on a five-note descending whole-tone scale fragment, and all the accompanying chords for the section are combinations of whole-tone intervals, an exquisitely subtle example of Debussy's use of whole-tone writing.)

A rapidly rising vocal line sung to a strong crescendo sweeps us to the climactic "la bouche sur la bouche"; this dramatic ascent is accompanied by a soaring arpeggio, a broadly rolled chord in the bass and powerfully pulsating chords in the treble.   A sudden *piano*, a return to the slow tempo of the beginning, and a subdued melodic line give a special flavor to the next line, the central image of the text: ""Ainsi que deux lauriers n'ont souvent qu'une racine." The voice pauses for a moment while the accompaniment resumes its measured chords. As the narrative continues, the pace

quickens again and another crescendo develops. This buildup
reaches its peak—the real climax of the song—at the end of "Ou
que tu entrais en moi comme mon songe."

At this point the narrator, having finished telling her story,
describes her reaction to her lover's passionate declaration.
Debussy creates a bridge between the two sections—so different in
mood—by bringing back the piano's introductory chords, a musical
analogue for the poet's "frame." In keeping with this "frame"
effect, the notes for "Quand il eut achevé" are the same as those
on which "Il m'a dit' were sung, and the piano and singer share
the melodic line for "il mit doucement ses mains sur mes épaules"
as they had for "Cette nuit j'ai rêvé."

The entire last section is sung in a mood of dazed tenderness
which is enormously poignant. The vocal line breaks off inconclu-
sively at the final word, "frisson," and the postlude repeats the
harmonies of the introductory bars in a hesitating, fragmented
fashion, both elements reflecting the inner turmoil aroused in the
narrator by her lover's naked passion. The final chord, played
after the slowly fading augmented penultimate harmony has been
allowed to die away, is an unambiguous G flat major. This might
be construed as Debussy's optimistic comment on the outcome of
this most intimate exposure of a lover's innermost—and hence most
vulnerable—being.

LE TOMBEAU DES NAIADES

> Le long du bois couvert de givre, je marchais;
> Mes cheveux devant ma bouche
> Se fleurissaient de petits glaçons,
> Et mes sandales étaient lourdes
> De neige fangeuse et tassée.
> Il me dit: "Que cherches-tu?"
> "Je suis la trace du satyre.
> Ses petits pas fourchus alternent
> Comme des trous dans un manteau blanc."
> Il me dit: "Les satyres sont morts.
> Les satyres et les nymphes aussi.
> Depuis trente ans, il n'a pas fait un hiver aussi terrible..
> La trace que tu vois est celle d'un bouc.

Mais restons ici, où est leur tombeau."
Et avec le fer de sa houe il cassa la glace
De la source où jadis riaient les naïades.
Il prenait de grands morceaux froids,
Et les soulevant vers le ciel pâle,
Il regardait au travers.

THE NAIADS' TOMB

Along the woods covered with frost, I walked;
My hair blown in front of my mouth
Blossomed with little icicles
And my sandals were heavy
With muddy and thick snow.
He said to me: "What are you looking for?
"I am following the satyr's tracks.
His little forked footprints alternate
Like holes in a white cloak." :
He said to me: "The satyrs are dead.
The satyrs and nymphs too.
For thirty years we have not had such a terrible winter.
The tracks you see are those of a buck.
But let us stay here at their tomb."
And with the iron of his hoe he broke the ice
Of the spring where naïads formerly laughed.
He took large cold pieces,
And raising them to the pale sky,
He looked through them.

In the overwhelming majority of Roman or Greek pastoral idylls, it is always summer; the usual Virgilian or Theocritan setting is that of an Arcadian never-never land, where shepherds, seeking shelter from the mid-day sun in which their flocks lazily graze, use their enforced leisure to sing, play their pipes and think of love. "Le Tombeau des naïades," however, presents a glacial winter scene. Since the earliest known pastorals set in winter landscapes occur in the Christian Era, and since the Island of Lesbos is hardly known for extended periods of sub-freezing weather, in "Le

Tombeau des naïades" Louÿs would have us assume that his Bilitis is a most imaginative innovator!

The language of Louÿs' prose-poem reflects the bleak frozen landscape in its technique as well as in its imagery. Not only are the woods covered with frost, the hair of the speaker frozen into icicles, and the snow thick and muddy, but the sentences are terse and the dialogue peremptory. The language is at first quite poetic: the placement of the subject and verb "je marchais" at the end of the first line is a poetic or at least rhetorical device, and the imagery of the icicles blossoming into little flowers on the speaker's windblown hair and the simile of the buck's tracks looking like holes in a white cloak are effective poetic devices. The wording becomes more matter-of-fact, however, as the text progresses. At the last four lines one once again feels poetic inspiration at work, but the ending seems unsatisfyingly abrupt.

The reader is told nothing about either of the two speakers except that the principal character, the person who "follows the trail of the satyr," is looking for the elusive demigod, and that the person he or she meets is masculine ("Il me dit"). Perhaps to offset the improbability of the frozen-tundra backdrop, Louÿs is careful to load "Le Tombeau des naïades" with the nymphs and satyrs of Greek mythology. Particularly clever is his casual reference to "mes sandales," for nineteenth-century Frenchmen did not wear sandals in the snow.

Debussy lavished a particularly interesting piano accompaniment on "Le Tombeau des naïades." The first bar introduces a slowly marching sixteenth-note figure—the equivalent of "walking music"—so we are not surprised when the singer announces that he or she has been walking in the frost-covered woods (Ex. I)

Although their pattern changes, steady sixteenth notes go on inexorably throughout the piece. Whenever the words speak of satyrs or nymphs, the sixteenth notes are combined with octaves in a way that makes them express frolicsome gaiety. Often in these sections the half-step interval between the two top notes of rolled chords in the piano part create a tinkling, bell-like sound (Ex. II).

But the brighter mood this establishes is always short-lived. In the piano interludes before "Il me dit" and after "Les satyres sont morts," the combined octaves and sixteenth notes sound bleak and full of despair.

Ex. I

Ex. II

All these changing moods are conveyed more strongly in the piano part than they are in the vocal line, which is in quasi-recitative style. The singer's first seven syllables, for example, are intoned on one note, and, after a rise to the major third above, they sink back to the original pitch. (Debussy's mood indication here is "gentle and weary.") In subsequent melodic phrases the singer is given more freedom and scope, but certain key lines—"Les satyres sont morts," for example—are again intoned on one pitch. At one point, when the second speaker somberly announces that the satyrs are dead, the accompaniment is still gaily imitating the sound one might associate with these amorally erotic

creatures of Greek mythology, indicating perhaps that the first
speaker is a bit slow to catch the import of his companion's
mournful words. Similar discrepancies occur from "Mais restons
ici" on, where the accompaniment is sometimes gayer than either
the vocal line or the text it is expressing would indicate. It is, of
course, the singular advantage of music to be able to present two
or more conflicting ideas and/or moods simultaneously. Here we
have both the sadness at the death of the satyrs and the joy their
memory brings to the two protagonists, who are now standing at
"la source où jadis riaient les naïades." In any case, the content
of the piano part is entirely appropriate to the purely musical
structure of the piece.

Debussy's way of coping with the abruptness of the final line of
text is to make a resounding climax of it—a solution, one must
conclude, based on musical rather than textual considerations. He
keeps the piano part interesting to the very end: the grace-notes
in the postlude are reminiscent of the bell-like sounds given to the
satyrs and its four short bars are full of dynamic contrast. The last
measure combines the tonic chord, F sharp major, with D sharp,
its relative minor.

Thanks to published correspondance between Debussy and Louÿs
(Librairie José Corti, 1945) and introductory comments by French
scholar Jean-Aubry, we have insights into both creators' thoughts
on these songs. We learn, for example, that the first segment of
Chansons de Bilitis to appeal to Debussy as a text was "La Flûte
de Pan," originally called "La Syrinx" by its author and listed as
number 20 in the Table of Contents. (Letter from Debussy to
Louÿs of May 10, 1897: "I should like very much to make
[*mélodies*] of the *Chansons de Bilitis*, among others the one
numbered 20. Would that please you and would it not incon-
venience you?") Louÿs was delighted with the idea and with the
finished product: "What you have done with my *Bilitis* is
adorablement bien," he wrote on July 8; "You cannot know how
much pleasure it gave me." By September of 1898 Debussy had
completed the three-song cycle: "Here are *Les Chansons de
Bilitis*," he wrote to Louÿs. "Better late than never."

The longest statement we have about the songs is found in a
letter from Debussy to Louÿs written in October of 1898, a month
before they were first sung in public and over a year before their

publication: "[the *Chansons de Bilitis*] contain, in marvelous language, everything that is ardently tender and cruel in the fact of being passionate, so much so, that the most subtly sensuous people are obliged to recognize the childishness of their games thanks to that terrible and charming Bilitis." Claiming that his music adds nothing to the texts, and even dilutes their emotional impact, he writes, "What good is it, really, to put Bilitis' voice to harmony, be it major or minor, since she already has the most persuasive voice in the world?"

But Debussy was wrong. "La Flûte de Pan" and "La Chevelure" are two of the most beautiful love songs in the repertoire, and, justly or not, *Les Chansons de Bilitis* and their author are remembered today principally through these exquisite musical evocations of her words.

Notes to Chapter VIII

1. Leopold Damrosch Jr., *Symbol and Truth in Blake's Myth* (Princeton University Press 1980) p. 363.
2. Charles Baudelaire, *Les Fleurs du Mal et autres poèmes* (Garnier-Flammarion, 1964, Edited by Henri Lemaître) p. 13.
3. Ibid., p. 14.

CHAPTER IX

GABRIEL FAURÉ

POÈME D'UN JOUR   Text by Charles Grandmougin

There are three parts to this singular "poem of a day," a beginning ("Rencontre"), a middle ("Toujours") and an end ("Adieu"). With its classic Aristotelian structure, it provides the text(s) for an indivisible song-cycle. The wry point of its finale is meaningless unless preceded by the other two sections, and its beginning and middle sections are deceivingly sentimental without its deflating dénouement.

The author of *Poème d'un jour*, Charles Grandmougin (1850-1930), is one of the least-known poets represented in the catalogue of songs by Fauré. Like Debussy, Fauré favored Paul Verlaine (there are seventeen Fauré songs based on Verlaine texts). Among Fauré's works are also found settings of poetry by Victor Hugo, Théophile Gautier, Charles Baudelaire, Leconte de Lisle and others of equal renown. Grandmougin is, however, not the only minor poet whose works attracted Fauré's attention, and a glance at the list of his collaborators reveals such unfamiliar names as Romain Bussine (famous at the time as a singer, translator of Italian dialect poetry, and cofounder with Camille Saint-Saëns of the Société Nationale de Musique), Louis Pomney, Paul Choudens and Marc Monnier. Fauré seemed to have the ability to discover what others had missed in poets not quite of the first rank. This was particularly the case with the French Symbolists Armand Sylvestre and Sully-Prudhomme, both of whom appear often among Fauré's settings, and above all with Belgian Symbolist Charles van Lerberghe, whose poems inspired two marvelous Fauré cycles, *La Chanson d'Eve* and *Le Jardin clos*.

There are three volumes of poetry by Grandmougin, *Les Siestes* of 1873, *Nouvelles poésies* of 1880, and *Poèmes d'amour* of 1884. These efforts were received by French critics with praise for their

author's language, which they called "à la fois très pure et très
colorée, très simple et très savante" (at the same time very pure
and very colorful, very simple and very knowledgeable). An essay
on Richard Wagner (1873), in which Grandmougin attempted to
evaluate the German composer without regard to political animosi-
ties resulting from the Franco-Prussian War of 1870, is a manifestation of his great love for music, which, he felt, should be above
all other considerations:

> En publiant cet opuscule, où je n'ai point caché ma
> grande   sympathie pour Wagner, je ne crois pas
> avoir failli au patriotisme.
> L'art est cosmopolite et le génie n'a point de
> patrie. J'estime qu'on doit admirer le beau partout
> où il se trouve.
> Ce n'est point en proscrivant les maîtres allemands
> que nous prendrons sérieusement notre revanche, car
> ce serait vraiment trop facile.
> Du reste, n'y a-t-il pas une certaine grandeur
> d'âme d'oublier ses ressentiments quand on est réuni
> sur le domaine de la musique?

> In publishing this treatise, in which I have not
> hidden my great sympathy for Wagner, I do not
> believe that I have failed to be patriotic.
> Art is cosmopolitan and genius has no homeland.
> I feel that one must admire the beautiful wherever it
> is found.
> It is not by outlawing the German masters that we
> shall seriously take our revenge, for that would truly
> be too easy.
> Besides, isn't there a certain greatness of soul in
> forgetting our resentments when we are united in
> the domain of music?

These citations from the preface to Grandmougin's *Esquisse sur
Richard Wagner* do not represent the popular point of view at the
time they were written, when France was still smarting from her
rapid defeat at Prussian hands in the ill-advised war which had so

recently ended, and Grandmougin showed considerable courage in expressing them.   He continued to write musical criticism, publishing an *Etude d'esthétique musicale* as late as 1900.

In his obituary notice in *La Nouvelle Revue*, Grandmougin is called "le dernier parnassien," the last of the Parnassians, evidence of his long association with this group of post-Romantic poets. At first glance the texts of *Poème d'un jour* do not seem to fit the description of Parnassian poetry, but if we interpret these verses as subtly expressed criticism of the typical Romantic protagonist—the interpretation most logical to this reader—their Parnassian point of view becomes clear.

RENCONTRE

J'étais triste et pensif quand je t'ai rencontrée:
Je sens moins, aujourd'hui, mon obstiné tourment.
O dis-moi, serais-tu la femme inespérée
Et le rêve idéal poursuivi vainement?

O passante aux doux yeux serais-tu donc l'amie
Qui rendrait le bonheur au poète isolé,
Et vas-tu rayonner, sur mon âme affermie,
Comme le ciel natal sur un coeur d'exilé?

Ta tristesse sauvage, à la mienne pareille,
Aime à voir le soleil décliner sur la mer!
Devant l'immensité ton extase s'éveille,
Et le charme des soirs à ta belle âme est cher.

Une mystérieuse et douce sympathie
Déjà m'enchaîne à toi comme un vivant lien,
Et mon âme frémit, par l'amour envahie
Et mon coeur te chérit sans te connaître bien.

MEETING

I was sad and pensive when I met you:
I feel less, today, my stubborn torment.
Oh tell me, could you be the woman I never hoped for
And the ideal dream vainly pursued?

Oh soft-eyed passer-by, could you then be the intimate
  friend
Who might bring happiness to the isolated poet,
And are you going to shine on my hardened soul,
Like the native sun on an exile's heart?

Your wild sadness, so like mine,
Likes to see the sun setting in the sea!
Your ecstasy awakens when confronted with infinity,
And the charm of evenings is dear to your beautiful soul.

A mysterious and sweet sympathy
Already ties me to you like a living bond,
And my soul trembles, invaded by love,
And my heart cherishes you without knowing you well.

In perfect alexandrines, each with its *césure* securely in place
after the sixth syllable, and with a rigidly regular alternating
end-sound rhyme scheme, Grandmougin gives us a devastating
portrait of the self-conscious Romantic poet. Because of his
isolation, due of course to his superiority, he feels an obstinate
torment; with his "sauvage" sadness (the French word may be
translated as wild, savage or shy) he prefers sunsets to sunrises,
the night to the day. The ideal woman he seeks but never really
hopes to find must match him in "tristesse" and in isolation.
Although he has just met the one to whom he is addressing these
impassioned remarks, he feels tied to her already by a sweet and
mysterious sympathy.

Gabriel Fauré was born in 1845. His musical gifts were recognized when he was quite young, and he was sent to study in Paris.
While still at L'Ecole Niedermeyer he met Saint-Saëns, who
introduced him to the works of Liszt and Wagner. By the time he
was twenty years old, he had published twenty songs and three
Songs Without Words for piano solo.

After graduating from L'Ecole Niedermeyer, Fauré worked as
an organist. He served in the army during the Franco-Prussian
War and later returned to Paris to teach at the school from which
he had graduated. He lived a quiet life, marked by the success of

some of his works (in particular the *Requiem*, still one of the most
frequently performed of his compositions) and the failure of others.
When not quite sixty years of age he began to grow deaf, and by
1920 he was forced to resign his position as Director of the
Conservatory.   Despite this handicap, several of his important
chamber works date from 1920 to 1924, the year of his death.

The music of Fauré is enormously subtle and original.   In such
haunting works as the "Tendresse" section of his *Dolly Suite* for
piano four-hands, for example, an endless stream of marvelous
modulations—worthy of comparison to the most magical moments
in Schubert—flows with "une nonchalance révolutionnaire" (a
revolutionary nonchalance);[1] in the opening "Berceuse" of that
same Suite, equally beautiful harmonic realizations are achieved
with the simplicity and purety of Bach or Mozart.   Fauré invented
a seemingly inexhaustible cache of substitutes for the usual V-I or
IV-I final cadence, arriving at the home tonality in "mille résolu-
tions exceptionnelles" (a thousand exceptional resolutions).[2]   Like
Debussy he sometimes favored strings of chords juxtaposed without
modulatory intervention, but it is in his freshly conceived—and
eternally freshly perceived—progressions that his music is at its
most beautiful.

Ex. I

Since "Rencontre" is the beginning of a three-part story, Fauré opens his setting of it with a simple introduction whose arpeggiated chords are asked to do no more than establish the song's moderate "walking" tempo and its D flat major (for Soprano or Tenor) tonality. The singer begins to tell his story with a simple descending scale fragment, but after the *césure* the melodic line sweeps back up to the original tonic note, falling back to the sub-median on the extended last syllable of "rencontrée" (Ex. I).

Generally, as it does in this first statement, although sometimes less obviously, Fauré's music matches the rhythm of the poem, creating long natural pauses for the singer at the end of each alexandrine and shorter breaks midway through. As the singer begins the second line of verse, a counter-melody, indicated by double-stemming the significant notes in the bass, is introduced in the accompaniment. This duet-like element recurs frequently throughout the song. The music for the first and third lines is the same, but—again following the scheme of the original poem—Fauré brings both melody and harmony to a more complete close after the fourth line of text than he had at the end of the second.

From the words "O passante aux doux yeux" at the beginning of the second stanza, the rising melodic line creates a musical analogue for the tension expressed by the singer's anxious questions. This tension continues to increase as the melody rises to a high A flat—the highest note in the song—at the climactic "soleil natal." Luigi Dallapiccola, in an article entitled "Words and Music in Italian Opera,"[3] expounds the theory that in the poetic quatrains used in Italian libretti "the emotional crescendo is always found in the third line." This verbal climax is duplicated in the music "through rhythmic animation or through a surprise of a harmonic nature or else through an upward movement of the melodic line."[4] After the climactic third line, there is a general decrescendo and release of musical and poetic tension. While it would be quite possible to argue that textually the emotional climax occurs in the third line of this second quatrain of "Rencontre," the music of the setting continues to build until the middle of its final line, diminishing only after the *césure*. Perhaps this is one of the many distinctions one might draw between the melodramatic Italian aria and the subtle *mélodie*.

A recapitulation of the brief piano introduction now leads to the second half of this essentially binary song. The words sung here, "Ta tristesse sauvage," which begin the third stanza, are marvelously alliterative, with their echoing t's and s's. At this repeat of the musical material, after the climactic rise to A flat at "Et mon coeur te chérit," the six syllable descent from the emotional and musical peak is extended by a fade-out postlude. Like the prélude, it consists of nothing more than broken tonic chords.

After the briefest of pauses, an angry, tumultuous, tempestuous outburst from the piano introduces "Toujours."

TOUJOURS

> Vous me demandez de me taire,
> De fuir de vous pour jamais
> Et de m'en aller, solitaire,
> Sans me rappeler qui j'aimais!
>
> Demandez plutôt aux étoiles
> De tomber dans l'immensité,
> A la nuit de perdre ses voiles,
> Au jour de perdre sa clarté!
>
> Demandez à la mer immense
> De désssecher ses vastes flots
> Et quand les vents sont en démence,
> D'apaiser ses sombres sanglots!
>
> Mais n'espérez pas que mon âme
> S'arrache à ses âpres douleurs,
> Et se dépouille de sa flamme
> Comme le printemps de ses fleurs!

ALWAYS

> You demand that I be silent,
> And fly from you forever

And go away, alone,
Without remembering the one I loved!

Rather tell the stars
To fall into the void,
And the night to lose its veils,
And the day to lose its light!

Tell the immense sea
To dry up its vast tides
And when the winds are wildly blowing
To still its sad sighs!

But do not hope that my soul
Will tear itself from its bitter pain,
And strip itself of its flame
As the Spring does its flowers!

Grandmougin's shift from the twelve-syllable lines of "Rencontre" to the eight-syllable verses of "Toujours" immediately
increases the pace of the poetry, from which we may gather that
things have moved quickly in our little drama as well.   Each
quatrain has but one principal verb—"demandez" in the first three
stanzas and "espérez" in the fourth—which further accelerates the
tempo, for this structure demands that each set of four lines be
read as one grammatical unit.   As the text tells us, the affair
between the soulful poet and the woman who matches him in
"tristesse sauvage" has not only begun, it already threatens to come
to an end.   But the ardent lover will not be dismissed; the stars
will fall from the skies, the night lose its mystery and the day its
clarity before he will leave his beloved, and his soul clings to its
bitter pain more fiercely than does fickle Spring to her flowers.
Such phrases as "s'arrache à ses âpres douleurs" echo in the
harshness of their sound the violent emotions of the protagonist, as
do the images of "sombres sanglots" and "vents en démence."
    Fauré's setting for "Toujours" is a continuous maëlstrom of
sound, with a relentless figure in the accompaniment either storm-

ing away or rapidly building to new climaxes after abrupt shifts to
piano (Ex. I)

Ex I

The voice enters with an accusation, beautifully dramatized by
Fauré's placement of the first syllable of the crucial word "demandez" on the downbeat of the third measure.   That the poet is
self-absorbed and self-pitying is underscored by Fauré's rise to a
held high note on "solitaire," a climactic moment perhaps more
telling than the weakly pathetic "qui j'aimais" at the end of the
section.   There is an abrupt shift in dynamics from the furious
forte to a *piano* at "Demandez plutôt aux étoiles," the beginning of
the second stanza, but no break in the headlong pace which
continues throughout the setting.

With each hyperbolic illustration of the lover's tenacity, the
music increases in volume and intensity, until we are once more at
full *forte*. The wildly metaphoric "vents en démence" brings the
vocal line to a piercing high F, followed, as the piano plays a
stormy countermelody, by an octave drop (Ex. II)

Ex II

The composer reminds both performers to keep the music *sempre forte* through "sombres sanglots," after which he permits a decrescendo. During the next section, "Mais n'espérez que mon âme," etc., there is another enormous *crescendo* which leads to the tempestuous ending. As he had in "Rencontre," Fauré follows the narrative content and metric scheme of "Toujours" quite carefully, pausing at the end of each line and emphasizing the poem's most telling images, but his extraordinary climax on the last phrase, "Comme le printemps de ses fleurs" is clearly determined by musical rather than poetic concerns. However it affects the balance of the text, this last grand musical gesture brings the song to a wonderful close (Ex. III).

Ex. III

ADIEU

Comme tout meurt vite, la rose
         Déclose,
Et les frais manteaux diaprés
         Des prés:
Les longs soupirs, les bien-aimées,
         Fumées!

On voit, dans ce monde léger,
       Changer
Plus vite que les flots des grèves
       Nos rêves,
Plus vite que le givre en fleurs,
       Nos coeurs!
A vous on se croyait fidèle,
       Cruelle,
Mais hélas! Les plus longs amours
       Sont courts!
Et je dis en quittant vos charmes,
       Sans larmes,
Presqu'au moment de mon aveu,
       Adieu!

FAREWELL

Since everything quickly dies, the rose
       Opens,
And the freshly variegated mantles
       Of the fields:
Long sighs, well-loved ones,
       Gone like smoke!
One sees, in this flighty world,
       Change
More quickly than the waves on the shores
       Our dreams,
More quickly than the flowering frost,
       Our hearts!
One believed oneself faithful to you,
       Cruel one,
But alas! the longest loves
       Are short!
And I say while leaving your charms,
       Without tears,
Almost at the moment of my vow,
       Adieu!

In this surprise ending to our three-part cycle, the protagonist has an abrupt change of heart: leaving his erstwhile beloved's charms with no regrets, at the very moment of his vows of eternal fidelity, he bids her a nonchalant "Adieu." His justifications are flowery evocations of natural phenomena—roses past their prime, the quickly melting patterns made by frost, the multicolored mantle briefly given to the fields by wild-flowers. Sooner or later—or rather sooner than later—all our dreams go up in smoke, he says, for the whole world is fickle ("ce monde léger"). His ability to project, as Freudian psychiatrists would define it, is prodigious—because he thought he could be faithful to her and cannot, in his mind *she* is the cruel one ("cruelle").

Grandmougin's design for this little poem is delightfully adroit: lines of eight syllables alternate with two-syllable verses, bringing the rhyming end-sounds startlingly close to one another. Those of the last four couplets, fidèle / Cruelle, amours / Sont courts, charmes / Sans larmes and aveu / Adieu, are particularly telling and amusing.

Fauré's setting provides some surprises too. After all the Romantic storm and stress of "Toujours," this last song begins with a quiet, rather innocuous introduction whose primarily four-part chords project an innocent and antique aura (Ex. I). The introductory figure, repeated once before the singer's entry and once again as the vocal part begins, is too bland to give much insight into what is about to happen, but we do have the sense that an oft-told tale rooted deep in the past is about to be told.

Ex. 1

Ex. II

The singer enters sweetly and guilelessly...who knows, perhaps the equally venerable "gather-ye-rosebuds-while-ye-may" message will follow the ominous analogy of rapidly fading blossoms. But no, the change in modality from major to minor for the piano's sadly lyric interlude after the singer's whispy rise on "Fumée" bodes ill.

Without changing the tempo, Fauré accelerates the perceived pace of the music as the poem speaks of our dreams changing more quickly than waves on the sand. He does this by allotting few syllables more than one sixteenth-note each and by pausing scarcely at all between "grèves" and "Nos rêves." (While Fauré provides a musical pause at the end of each couplet, he varies greatly—and to great effect—the degree of separation between the long and short lines.) The climax of this middle section in the essentially A B A song is on the next couplet, "Plus vite que le givre en fleurs, / Nos coeurs!"; long held notes on "fleurs" and "Nos coeurs," followed by a brief piano interlude in which a slight retard seems natural, bring us back to the original, calmer movement.

There are small but significant changes in the accompaniment at the beginning of the recapitulation. Chords which were originally played as one are now broken into two alternating units, the bass and treble are phrased quite differently, and both staccato and legato touches are used. Even more significant are the differences in the vocal line, where minute rhythmic changes—the upbeat-downbeat arrangement of "A vous" and the sixteenth-note rest before "Cruelle"—help clarify the meaning of the words (Ex. II).

Since the ironic juxtaposition of "en quittant vos charmes / Sans larmes" is so important and so difficult to catch, the singer must stretch the sixteenth-note pause between the two lines just enough to make sure the words are understood.

The composer takes no chances with his setting for the poem's punch lines, "Presq'au moment de mon aveu / Adieu!": for these words he writes a new melodic line to a new accompaniment in a new key. To assure maximum effect he allots three full beats to the second syllable of "aveu," and then writes an eighth-note rest before allowing the singer to deliver, still sweetly and ever so softly, the final "Adieu." By this time the music has worked its way back to the home base so that the postlude can conclude with two whole measures of very definite, very final, very banal tonic chords. The protagonist's flowery statements have not deceived us.

Notes to Chapter IX

1. *Cinquante ans de musique française,* p. 23.
2. Ibid.
3. *The Verdi Companion* edited by William Weaver and Martin Chuzid (Norton, 1979) pp. 198-202.
4. Ibid., p. 202.

Chapter X

GEORGES AURIC

ALPHABET   poetry by Raymond Radiguet

Most listeners would agree with French musicologist Charles Koecklin[1] that the late nineteenth, early twentieth-century French mélodie, as exemplified by the settings of Debussy, Duparc, Fauré and Chausson of texts by such poets as Verlaine, Baudelaire, Leconte de Lisle, Maeterlinck and Mallarmé, was more aristocratic and further removed from mass culture than its counterpart, the German lied.   By and large (needless to say there are always exceptions) the marvelous lieder of Schubert, Schumann, Brahms and their contemporaries could be related to at least some elements of the Germanic folk tradition: their vocal lines were often tuneful, sometimes even hummable; more than occasionally they were strophic settings of reasonably accessible poetry and even when through-composed, the strophic nature of their poetic texts usually remained apparent. Most important, however original and evocative their music was, they remained rhythmically and harmonically within the grasp of the average music lover.

This cannot be said of the hauntingly ephemeral, infinitely subtle mélodies of the French post-Romantic masters which, consequently, have always appealed to a far smaller audience. It would be absurd to look for folk elements in either the poem or the music of a Duparc-Baudelaire song like "L'Invitation au voyage" or a Debussy-Verlaine opus like "Colloque sentimental" for example; these exhale the rarified atmosphere of the remote, the suggested, the veiled, an atmosphere that by 1900 was generally thought of as uniquely French.

Jean-Paul Sartre had an explanation for the advent of this peculiarly elevated French style, so different from that of the first generation of French Romantic poets and the composers (Berlioz,

Bizet, Gounod) who set their words to music. In his opinion, to
Lamartine (1790-1869), Alfred de Vigny (1797-1863) and the young
Victor Hugo (1802-1885), poetry had a divine function; "the poet
read the Truth in the stars...No one questioned such things as
absolute Truth, Beauty and Good; no one doubted the Poet's
Mission."[2] This sense of purpose, agreed upon by the writer and
the reader, tied the poet to the real world and brought him a large
and sympathetic audience.

Sometime between 1830 and 1850, at least partially because of
the unsuccessful revolutions that took place during those years and
the concomitant stranglehold of the bourgeoisie on all aspects of
French society, the French creative artist became disoriented and
alienated. Furthermore, what many have seen as the "death of
God" occurred at this very same time, leaving the artist without the
familiar signs of his innate superiority to the despised class from
which he had sprung.

"When people still basked in faith," writes Sartre, "the gift of
poetry had been the sign of the natural aristocrat. God had placed
his seal on the brows of the elect; one was a poet by divine
will...In short the poet was only the trumpet; God supplied the
breath...with the death of God, sacred delirium becomes just
another kind of quirky obsession...[3] With the absence of God in
Heaven as on Earth and the bourgeoisie firmly in control, the
creative artist could no longer assume a connection to reality.
"From 1850 to the early twentieth century, from the post-Romantic
generation to the last Symbolists, writing meant exile [Victor Hugo
was actually in exile, at first government imposed and then
self-inflicted, from 1852 to 1870]. To write was to engage in an
activity external to life."[4]

As long as Victor Hugo was alive, poet and populace were
never totally divorced, but gradually the gap that had begun in the
1850's widened to a chasm, with poetry becoming ever more
esoteric and readership becoming ever smaller. It was perhaps
inevitable that the pendulum should swing back, however, and
World War I brought to a climax a reversal in the aesthetic
atmosphere in France which had been brewing since the turn of the
century.

Suddenly there seemed to be a collapse of the old intellectual
order. The most rational disciplines were rocked by a general

sense of arbitrariness and absurdity, the result of four years of a ferocious, deadly, and—as history was to prove—futile war (ten percent of all French soldiers were killed in World War I, thousands of others horribly wounded). Exquisite refinement, heretofore thought of as quintessentially French, gave way to an earthy, bawdy gaiety which was more closely related to the cabaret than the Académie, and all art forms were affected. With the revolutionary cubism of Picasso, Braque and Juan Gris, paintings no longer had fixed points of view, a departure from academic painting more radical even than that which had been wrought by the Impressionists; with the endless punning and seemingly meaningless juxtapositions of words in the poetry of Surrealists and Dadaists, literature, like cubism, became "a succession of changing planes of meaning," justified, if at all, by connections whose logic was apparent only to its creators.[5]

As art changed, so did the artists. Their lives became public manifestations of, or sometimes substitutes for, their aesthetic production. They used personal scandal to keep their ideas in the public eye; they sought bizarre experience to whet their imaginations, to create images unsummonable by logic or simple reverie. They drank to excess, used drugs, experimented with all possible sexual combinations, and talked about all of it without the slightest trace of *pudeur*. They ate, worked and socialized in public cafés instead of at home or in private salons. They formed groups, collaborated, quarreled, reconciled, quarreled again. In Roger Shattuck's words, they created "an atmosphere of permanent explosion."[6]

French music had to be shaken up too. Schönberg and Stravinsky had already turned the musical world upside down, the former with the deliberate dissolution of traditional tonality in the piano pieces of Opus 11 and the fifteen songs from Stefan George's *Buch der hängenden Gärten*, Opus 15 (1908). The latter did so with the polyharmonies and atavistic rhythms of *Firebird* (1910), *Petrouchka* (1911) and, of course, the riot-provoking *Rite of Spring* (1913). But, having recently fought so desperately against the all-pervasive influence of Richard Wagner, the French were hardly amenable to being led by another German-speaking composer (Schönberg was of course Viennese), nor did they seem naturally predisposed to anything as abstract as atonality. They were more receptive to the innovations of Stravinsky, who, although born in Russia had the good taste to prefer Paris; but French musicians were too chauvinistic to want their new music to take its inspiration exclusively from him.   Nevertheless the subtlety of Impressionistic music could not continue to prevail: "Enough of clouds, waves, aquariums, water-nymphs and fragrances wafted at night," wrote Jean Cocteau, testily denouncing Saint-Saëns, Debussy and all other composers who in his opinion were guilty of "indulging in liquid sonorities."[7]

In May of 1917 Cocteau and company provoked their own riot, with a theatre piece called *Parade*. Cocteau was at the helm of this collaborative venture, which he dubbed "a cubist manifesto"; Picasso painted the scenery, Massine did the choreography, and Erik Satie composed the music. Explaining that he wanted to created "un tapis résonnant" for the choreography, Satie wrote music whose sparsely orchestrated, monotonously repeated linear phrases are set to distinctive rhythmic patterns which create a symmetical structure.   Some of those rhythmic patterns were derived from Afro-American jazz, which, as Satie said, "shouts its sorrows,"[8] but the really disturbing element in the music is the way in which Satie deprives ordinary melodic fragments and simple harmonies of their traditional associations. In a way, by reintegrating commonplace musical elements into unexpected patterns, Satie was echoing musically what the cubist painters were doing visually, justifying Cocteau's rubric.[9]

In a charming article in *La Nouvelle Revue Française* Georges Auric, whose tiny song-cycle *Alphabet* will be the focus of the following discussion, tells us why *Parade* fascinated him and his contemporaries: "Cocteau a présenté *Parade* ainsi qu'un gros jouet, simple comme 'bonjour'..." (Cocteau presented *Parade* like a big plaything, as simple as 'hello'). In explanation of youth's attraction to what seemed merely vulgar to the traditionalists he says, "Le 'Jazz-Band' ou le 'Cirque' sont aussi ennuyeux que les cathédrales et les couchers de soleil. Mais qu'on y découvre moins de prétention . . ." (The 'Jazz-Band' or 'Circus' are just as boring as cathedrals and sunsets but one discovers less pretension in them). In any case one must always look for new ideas: "On s'ennuyerait trop vraiment à récrire l'*Ode à la joie*" (One would really be too bored if one rewrote *The Ode to Joy*).

Inspired by the irreverence, novelty and lack of pretension of
Parade, a whole covey of young composers began to regard Satie,
who was born in 1866, as their master and mentor. "Satie, c'était
l'ordre, la raison, la clarté...Il nous a appris à tous une simplicité
inconnue..." (Satie was order, reason, clarity ... he taught us an
unknown simplicity) wrote Auric.[10] Six disciples, later dubbed
"Les Six" after the famous Russian "Five," became particularly
close to Satie and to one another. These young Turks were
Francis Poulenc, Louis Durey, Germaine Tailleferre, Darius
Milhaud, Arthur Honegger, and Auric himself. Intensely individu-
alistic, these composers did not long remain a cohesive force, if
indeed they ever really were one. Their sole collaborative effort
was for the 1920 production of *Les Mariés de la Tour Eiffel*, after
which they went their own ways. Poulence and Auric did however
remain close friends; to Satie's dismay they also retained their love
for Stravinsky, who chose them as the two permanent members of
the piano quartet for which his ballet *Les Noces* is scored (the
other two pianists varied).[11]

One of the traits for which Satie was most noted was his
iconoclastic sense of humor. It was reflected in the titles he chose
for his compositions such as "Trois morceaux en forme de poire"
(Three pieces in the shape of a pear) for piano duet and
"Embryons desséchés" (Dessicated embryos) for piano solo, and
in the odd-ball instructions he wrote with seeming seriousness to
the performers of his music.

Like so many other creative members of his generation, Georges
Auric (1899-1983) had always been attracted to the humorous in
music, in literature, and in life: "Il est vain de s'expliquer sur le
Comique. *Parsifal*, la *Messe en ré* me paraissent d'un énorme
comique" (You can't explain your view of the Comic. *Parsifal*,
the D minor Mass seem enormously comic to me), he wrote in the
article quoted above, as though challenging the reader to deny such
an outrageous, deadpan statement. A product of the Conservatoire
and d'Indy's Schola Cantorum in Paris and an early admirer of
Maurice Ravel, Auric found his true mentors in Satie and Stravinsky. After 1932, the year of his great success as the composer of
the score for the René Clair film *A nous la liberté*, Auric became
more and more involved in the French and English cinema.
Caesar and Cleopatra of 1945, *Passport to Pimlico* of 1949,

Lavender Hill Mob of 1951 were among his many extremely popular movies. But in 1920, the year he composed *Alphabet*, he was still closely tied to the world of Francis Picabia's dadaesque can\ es, Diaghilev's controversial ballets and Jean Cocteau's absurdist theatre pieces. All of these arenas, as well as his friendship and collaboration with Raymond Radiguet (1903-1923), the poet whose texts are set in *Alphabet*, allowed Auric full rein for his comic sensibilities.

As Freud made clear, humor, like "dream-work," is a form of thought which relies on compression: syntactical links—the "buts" and "becauses" of logic, the cadential modulations of music—are skipped; syllogistic resolutions are replaced by laughter-provoking surprises. Humor embraces ambiguity. By encouraging multiplicity of meaning in any given word—the antithesis of the Racinian or Flaubertian goal of "le mot juste" (the exactly right word)—it raises the pun to the status of a legitimate literary method.[12] Humor eschews monumental size, demanding economy of expression; it allows apparent confusion of meaning, resists consistency and convention. It favors the popular, demands an alertness to the present moment, and is the perfect vehicle for a phenomenon which had first appeared on the artistic scene in the person of Arthur Rimbaud, the "child-man," the artist who refuses to put off childish things and insists on retaining the child's sense of wonder and spontaneity. Even the infantile tendency toward destructiveness is seen by the "child-man" and those who esteem him as a positive trait, one to be treasured and nurtured rather than outgrown. The familiar "sois sage" (be wise) is thus transmuted to an indulgent "sois sauvage" (be wild).

When Auric and Radiguet met, they would have qualified as "child-men" even without the poses they affected, for that is really what they were. Radiguet, a gaunt, undersized, extremely myopic boy with a mop of unruly hair and an incongruous monocle[13] was barely out of short pants when the journal *Sic* accepted his first pieces. Auric too had had his first compositions, as well as a sensitive article on Satie, published when he was not quite fifteen years old. Both had immediately been welcomed into the comradeship of the avant-garde (Satie went to call on this unknown M. Auric who had praised him with such understanding in Léon Vallas' revue, and, "ravi d'avoir découvert un disciple de quatorze

ans," (delighted to have discovered a fourteen-year old disciple)
treated him with all the dignity due to an adult cohort).[14] Both
Auric and Radiguet became involved in premature sexual initiation
and hard drinking. Radiguet, in fact, was only fourteen years old
when he had an affair with the wife of a soldier who was fighting
at the front in World War I, an experience which led to his
shocking and highly praised novel, *Le Diable au corps*. (In the
novel he makes the protagonist 16, feeling perhaps that readers
would find it too difficult to believe that a mature married woman
could be swept off her feet by a fourteen year old boy.)

By the time he wrote *Diable*, which was published in 1923, the
year of his death, Radiguet had more or less renounced both poetry
and his early avant-garde aesthetic. Instead he aimed for, and in
the novel mostly achieved, a pure classicism based on such early
French masterpieces as Madame de La Fayette's *La Princesse de
Clèves*. But from 1915 to 1920, the years in which all his poems
were written, Radiguet was as caught up in the humorous antics of
the period as Cocteau, his principal mentor and lover, or Auric,
his good friend.

Auric was four years Radiguet's senior, and he might have acted
as a restraining influence on the younger adolescent. Instead he
allowed his appreciation of the ridiculous to override common
sense: "Cocteau and Radiguet formed a pair of inseparables whom
we never grew tired of watching, Georges Auric and I," writes
Jacques Porel in *Fils de Réjane*. "We would observe him with
women and with alcohol. [Radiguet was bisexual, and had many
affairs with women, but evidently no homosexual lovers other than
Cocteau. He confided to Auric his dismay that all the women who
made themselves available to him turned out to be virgins: "Je le
voyais revenir effondré, terrorisé: C'est épouvantable . . . c'était
encore une vierge," (I saw him return devestated, terrorized: It's
horrible...she was still a virgin) he told Auric.[15] We came very
close to encouraging him [from excess to excess]. It was a
dangerous game.[16] Indeed it was a fatal game, for Radiguet died
on December 12, 1923, at the age of 20, from typhoid fever. It
was a death that might have been avoided had he not been so
weakened by dissipation. He left behind the manuscript of a
second novel, *Le Bal du Comte d'Orgel*. Laboriously and lovingly
typed by Auric, it was subsequently edited by Cocteau and

published to great acclaim. There were also plans for a collection of all his poetry to be issued under the title *Les Joues en feu*, the name he had already used for his first published collection, a volume of fourteen poems which had appeared in July of 1920.

The seven quatrains which compose the text for *Alphabet* are culled from two series, both of which may be found in the complete *Les Joues en feu*. "Bateau," "Filet à papillons" and "Hirondelle" are taken from the first group, which is called *Lettres d'un alphabet*; the second group, entitled simply *Alphabet*, and published earlier (1921) in Radiguet's second collection, *Devoirs de vacances*, gives us "Album," "Domino," "Escarpin" and "Mallarmé". There are nineteen other little poems in the two cycles. The last, "Zéro," is too endearing not to quote:

> Lectrice, adorable bourreau,
> Plus que jamais soyez sévère
> Quand vous découvrez ces vers
> A peine dignes d'un zéro.

> Reader, lovable executioner,
> Be more severe than ever
> When you discover these verses
> ·Scarcely worthy of a zero.

But our *Alphabet* starts with "A," not "Z," so let us begin at the beginning.

I. ALBUM

> Apprendre n'est pas un pensum
> Lectrice qui ne savez lire
> Ayez grand soin de cet album
> Né du plus funeste délire.

I. ALBUM

> Learning isn't an onerous task
> Reader who doesn't know how to read

Be very careful with this album
Born of the most funereal delirium.

So much of this little poem is reminiscent of childhood! We
have the teacher encouraging the reader who cannot yet read by
telling him it's not really so hard to learn; the use of the Latin
word "pensum," which might come from a required vocabulary
list; and the age-old mnemonic device of poems as illustrations of
the letters of the alphabet. Indeed, everything about "Album,"
including the very title of the collection in which the verses
originally appeared (*Homework to be done during vacation*), is
designed to evoke the world of the schoolboy.

Since Radiguet was sixteen at the most when he wrote the poem,
its closeness to childhood is not surprising. What is remarkable is
its sophistication and skill. Its brevity, its gaiety and the banality
of its subject might cause the casual reader to overlook the way in
which its author, in regular octosyllabic lines, uses sounds (the
multiple alliteration of "pas un pensum") and rhythms (the
weightiness of "plus funeste" immediately countered by the
lightness of "délire") to make the poem sparkle. Nor should one
ignore the mock seriousness of the paradoxical and incongruous
last line—"Born of the most funereal delirium" —which, by the
way, rolls around in one's mouth quite as wonderfully in English
as it does in the original! Fortunately none of these charming and
witty features escaped the notice of Georges Auric.

As is true in all seven sections of *Alphabet*, the musical setting
of "Album" expands the duration of the poem with several
measures of introduction, interlude and postlude for piano solo.
The first letter of the alphabet obviously merits its musical
counterpart—C major or "Do" as the French are more likely to
think of it—so Auric begins and ends his setting with C major
chords. Immediately after the opening chord, however, wildly
unrelated harmonies appear, after which the tonalities never cease
to jump about in a carefree, anti-academic manner. Only the 3/4
waltz-time meter remains constant, creating a swinging,
nonchalant, cabaret atmosphere. Mock-ominous trills in the
accompaniment underscore the vocal line at "Né du plus funeste
délire," but the jaunty tempo and persistent waltz-time negate any

possible uneasiness. The little piece is over so quickly that the
listener is hard put to catch hold of its details, but its whimsical
mood is unmistakable. Since the vocal line is consistently echoed
by one part or another in the accompaniment, the accessibility of
the cabaret song is achieved, but the delightfully quirky harmonic
touches in the piano part lend a sophistication that sustains interest
even after multiple hearings.   In the introduction alone, for
example, we have a B major figure following the opening C major
chord, that figure's subsequent resolution to C sharp, which
immediately yields to D minor, and a descending D flat major
scale which resolves to a "vamp until ready" pattern rooted in G.
(Ex. I)

Ex. I

Ex. II

The postlude, while much shorter than the prelude, has its own harmonic bravura, for after singer and accompanist have settled into what seems to be a solid C major conclusion, two polytonal surprises remain to be savored by the listener (Ex II.)

II. BATEAU

Bateau debout, bateau hagard
La danseuse sans crier gare
Sans même appeler les pompiers
Mourut sur la pointe des pieds.

II. BOAT

Upright boat, haggard boat
The dancer, scarcely crying
Without even calling the fire department
Died on the tip of her toes.

This is one of Radiguet's most dadaesque poems, and it would be foolishly pedantic to try to force a logical statement from it. The only observation one might offer is that the first line seems totally divorced from the other three, which are related—however nonsensically—in narrative function. The knowledge that Radiguet was constantly being compared to that earlier enfant-terrible of French literature, Arthur Rimbaud, an association he rejected and resented, makes one think of its opening words, "Bateau debout," as a sort of facetious rebuttal of Rimbaud's famous major opus, *Bateau ivre*.

For his setting, Auric divides the poem in two sections, giving fully half the song to the first line, then putting the remainder of the quatrain in the second part. This appropriately emphasizes the complete break in text between the first line and the other three. The entire first half, which consists of fourteen measures, only four of which include the singer, is a marvelous tango, replete with delicious "wrong note" harmonies. (Ex. I) The tango itself was newly arrived (circa 1915) in Europe as a ballroom dance from Argentina, its African origins having been more or less obliterated

during its long sojourn on Latin American soil. It was all the rage
in Paris during the 1920's, and Auric exploits its sultry rhythm in
an amusing manner.

Since in its eight syllables of text the melodic line more or less
duplicates the upper voice of the piano part, the entire first section
could stand as a piano solo.

Ex. I

As the text changes character, so does the music: the three flats
of the opening C minor key signature are erased to make way for
C major, and the original "Mouvement de Tango" instruction is
replaced by "Mouvement de Mazurka." Here the piano and singer
have separate but equal parts to play, the accompanist's left hand
providing a steady 3/4 beat under the singer's long melodic notes
while his right hand plays a quirky tune of its own which is placed
high in the tinkly upper reaches of the keyboard. All forces are
united on C major from the last syllable of text until the piano's
final, mildly subversive, augmented chord.

III. DOMINO

> Domino jeu des ménages
> Embellit les soirs de campagne
> Du grand-père écoutons l'adage:
> Qui triche enfant finit au bagne.

III. DOMINO

> Dominoes, family game,
> Embellishes evenings in the country
> Let's listen to the grandfather's adage:

He who cheats as a child winds up breaking rocks on a chain gang.

This little quatrain must evoke a nostalgic smile from anyone who has ever spent a long evening *en famille* in the country, whiling away the time with chess, checkers, puzzles or dominoes. And who does not recognize old Grandpa, admonishing his young adversaries against cheating, while perhaps not above a little "tricherie" himself if the going gets tough enough!

Auric's setting is once again enormously entertaining. It enlarges and embellishes the text with brief interludes for piano solo, introduces Grandpa's adage with an attention-getting flourish, and underscores the word "bagne" with a saucy glissando (accepted slang for the harshest prisons, "bagne" is derived from *le bain*, the bath; according to *Le Petit Larousse*, the term arose because work in one such prison was carried out in caves below sea level). The opening measures suggest a military march, while the jaunty syncopations in the bars accompanying the second line of verse would not be out of place in a cabaret song. As is the case in each of these seven settings, the song is over before you know it— as brief and punchy as the wit of its text demands.

IV. FILET AU PAPILLONS

"Papillon, tu es inhumain!
Je te poursuis depuis hier,"
Ainsi parlait une écolière
Que j'ai rencontrée en chemin.

IV. THE BUTTERFLY NET

"Butterfly, you are inhuman!
I have been following you since yesterday,"
Thus spoke a schoolgirl
I met on the road.

The pun on "inhumain," the petulance of the schoolgirl at the butterfly's refusal to cooperate in its own capture, the cleverly harmonious end-rhymes, the inner rhyme of "poursuis/depuis," the insouciant ending to the anecdote—all these factors add up to another beguiling quatrain.   Auric captures the flightiness of schoolgirl, butterfly and poetry with a light-weight piano part composed primarily of even sixteenth notes. The accompaniment rarely goes lower than middle C, and although the tessitura of the vocal line is not particularly high, it skips along airily, intertwining with the piano's sixteenth-note figures. The melody for the last line of text is in cabaret style, and the piano's whimsical finale floats off into space. (Ex. I)

Ex. I

V. MALLARMÉ

> Un éventail qui fut l'oiselle
> Exquise des rudes étés
> Effleure fraîchement de l'aile
> L'oiseau sur la tasse à thé.

MALLARMÉ

> A fan which was the exquisite
> Bird of difficult summers
> Cordially brushes with its wing
> The bird on the teacup.

Without its title this poem would make no sense at all, but, taking advantage of the clue offered by the poet and hence glancing at the three poems by Stéphane Mallarmé set to music in 1913 by Claude Debussy (certainly known to Radiguet and Auric in both original and *mélodie* form), we find some basis for an explication.

As Jean-Paul Sartre explains, Mallarmé wanted to free ordinary words for poetic use by prying them loose from their usual concrete referents. To allow for the "rapid oscillation between possibilities of meaning..." which he felt necessary for the creation of poetic truth, Mallarmé had to defamiliarize language by "... assaulting the petrified façade of established discourse..."[17] This he does in many poems, including "Placet futile" and "L'Eventail," the second and third of Debussy's *Trois Chansons de Mallarmé*.

The language of these beautiful poems is so ambiguous, so opaque, that any précis is at best a weak approximation and—in its attempt to imprison the poetic vocabulary within the confines of narrative logic—a falsification. Nevertheless, some vague idea of content can be essayed. In the first of the two poems, an Abbé is unsuccessfully petitioning a beautiful blond princess. He envies everything that comes into contact with his haughty beloved—her little lap dog, her makeup, even Hébé, the Greek goddess painted on the Sèvres china teacup which she touches with her lips:

> Princesse! à jalouser le destin d'une Hébé
> Qui poind sur cette tasse au baiser de vos lèvres.

> Princess! to be jealous of the fate of an Hébé
> Who sprouts on this cup at the kiss of your lips.

He himself is such a lowly person, continues the poor Abbé, that he "ne figurerai même nu sur le Sèvres" (wouldn't even figure nude on the Sèvres). Among the images conjured up later on in the poem is "Amour, ailé d'un Eventail" (Love, winged with a Fan).

In the second poem the protagonist commands his dreamy loved one to know how, by a subtle lie, to keep his wing in her hand:

> O rêveuse, pour que je plonge
> Au pur délice sans chemin,

Sache, par un subtil mensonge,
Garder mon aile dans ta main.

Oh dreamer, for me to plunge
Into the pure pathless delight
Know, through a subtle lie,
How to keep my wing in your hand.

By the second verse—and with a hint from the title—we surmise
that the speaker is a fan. He makes space tremble like a kiss

Qui, fou de naître pour personne,
Ne peut jaillir ni s'apaiser

Which, mad with having been born for no one,
Can neither burst forth nor quiet down.

"Do you sense what a ferocious paradise runs from the corner
of your mouth into my folds when you hide a laugh?" he asks. He
calls himself "ce blanc vol fermé" (this closed, white flight) and
pictures himself placed "contre le feu d'un bracelet" (against the
fire of a bracelet).

Radiguet's verses do no more than suggest the far more significant works of Mallarmé, but how delightfully they do so!
Oblivious to the French reluctance to accept neologisms, he invents
the word "oiselle," a compendium perhaps of *oiseau* and *mademoi-
selle*, which gives him a light, airy sound as well as the rhyme he
wants.

The vocal line and accompaniment of Auric's setting -- warm
and a bit sentimental as Debussy's most certainly never are -- seem
more closely tied to one another than they are in the preceding
sections of *Alphabet*. As though to counter the opaqueness of the
text, the music is simple and straightforward, beginning in G
minor, ending in G major. The singer's last five syllables, sung
to the first five notes of the ascending G scale, are echoed by the
piano's final figure, and for once the concluding tonality is
uncomplicated by extraneous tones. There is nothing really
humorous about this little song—it's just sweet and pretty.

VI. HIRONDELLE

Comme chacun sait l'hirondelle
Annonce la belle saison
Elle n'a pas toujours raison
Mais nous croyons en elle.

VI. SWALLOW

As everyone knows the swallow
Announces the beautiful season
She's not always right
But we believe in her.

Of the seven songs in *Alphabet*, "Hirondelle" seems most like a nursery-song in both music and text. To extend the tiny poem Auric once again writes a relatively substantial introduction—three lighthearted, jaunty measures (Ex. I).

Ex. I

The only discordant note in the piece—an F sharp against an F natural—occurs in the accompaniment to the words "la belle saison," and it's a mild and quickly forgotten dissonance at that. The sassy way in which the piano and voice toss off the final words is very much in cabaret style.

VII. ESCARPIN

Grand bal dans la forêt ce soir
Les dryades à chaque pin
Ont accroché deux escarpins
Que chaussent leurs cavaliers noirs.

VII. DANCING PUMPS

Grand ball in the forest tonight
The dryads on each pinetree
Have hung two dancing pumps
Which their black cavaliers wear.

In this poem Radiguet eschews witticisms and obscure references in favor of sheer description, and what a charmingly picturesque fantasy he conjures up! Why do the dryads hang their dark cavaliers' elegant patent-leather dancing shoes on branches of pine trees? Radiguet doesn't say, but the image assures us that we are in a benign forest, one in which dragons and monsters have no place.

Like Ravel's *Mother Goose Suite*, which was written some ten years before *Alphabet* and which might very well have inspired at least some of its sections, Auric's setting for "Escarpin" evokes the poem's gentle world of make-believe. The composer instructs the pianist to "envelope" the introductory chords in what Poulenc elsewhere called "a halo of pedal," undoubtedly to veil the imagery with the musical equivalent of hazy forest light. Although the meter is 4/4 rather than waltz or minuet time, one senses the swaying movement of an ephemeral dance. The four-flat key signature of the little piece suggests F minor as the principal tonality, but Auric's avoidance of the median tone of the triad (it first appears at the end of the third measure) and the tone-cluster-like off-beat chords in the first two bars obscure the minor modality (Ex. I)

As befits the impalpable air created by the words, the penultimate measures of the piano part oscillate between F major and minor, finally closing on the open F / C interval mysteriously colored by a B flat. (Ex. II) This is just the sort of indeterminate, free-floating end-sound Poulenc loved, and it proves a perfect finish to this charmingly, deliberately inconsequential cycle.

Ex. I

Ex. II

Alphabet has not held a place in either the mélodie or the chanson repertoire—the only performance of it for which we have found documentation was in 1921 as part of a special event at Pierre Bertin's *Théâtre Bouffe*; there it shared billing with *Le Piège de Méduse*, a one-act play with music by Satie, and a shimmy composed by Darius Milhaud for *Le Nègre Gratin*. Yet we have chosen to include it in a study which purports to concentrate on the most important examples of the art song literature. Why?

For one thing, we find the cycle absolutely delightful and unjustly neglected. Then too it is a perfect example of the kind of music, poetry, and combination thereof that defines the 1920's in France.

Like so many of Radiguet's poems, the quatrains of *Alphabet* are "une sorte de retour à l'enfance, avec le raffinement malgré tout, de qui ne se laisse prendre qu'à demi...un mélange curieux, paradoxal, d'humeur conscient et d'instinctive candeur"[18] (a kind of return to childhood, with the refinement in spite of everything, of that which allows itself to be only partially grasped...a curious and paradoxical mixture of conscious humor and instinctive candor). Written by an adolescent, Radiguet's poems are the natural expression "de pudeur, de cachotterie propre à l'âge auquel ils ont été écrits" (of modesty, of secrecy about things of little importance appropriate to the age at which they were written), wrote Radiguet in the preface he had prepared for the Grasset edition of *Les Joues en feu*.

With their regular meter and their neat end-rhymes ("mes vers sont rimés quand cela me chante," [my verses are rhymed when that sings to me] he said) Radiguet's poems point the way to the classicism their author was to embrace in his two novels, but their subject matter remains that of the post-World War I avant-garde—the banal, the suggestive, the fantastic and the humorous. That these tiny verses succeed as poetry at all may be attributed to their transparency. As one admirer of *Les Joues en Feu* comments, they are "esquisses en plein air, en plein vol...des bribes de conversation ou de paysage..."[19] (sketches made out-of-doors, in full flight...snatches of conversation or of landscape) Only its tone transforms Radiguet's language, which is a montage of clichés and dislocations of the everyday, into poetry,[20] although for some it is l'esprit plus que la poésie, qu'y sourit aimablement" (it is wit, rather than poetry, that smiles amiably therein).[21]

"Bantering wit [raillerie] is so natural to M. Auric," wrote a contemporary critic,[22] "that one never knows whether, at the same time, he does not judge the same phrase to be simultaneously charming and ridiculous." Perhaps because he couldn't keep a straight face long enough (although this didn't bother Haydn!) Auric was never attracted to "Les Grandes Formes" of composition. "J'attendis des années avant d'achever une sonate" (It took me years to finish one sonata), he wrote.[23] Instead he dreamed "de brefs ouvrages où se confondraient danses et chants," (of short works in which dances and songs would be mixed together). His friendship with Radiguet and his delight in his younger cohort's pert poems gave him the perfect vehicles for his particular talent.

Because of the brevity of Radiguet's "exquisitely banal" texts[24] and the completeness of the piano parts in Auric's settings, unless the singer takes the time and trouble to articulate each word as carefully as he or she would in a Gilbert and Sullivan patter-song, the poetry is easily eclipsed by the music in *Alphabet*. The music itself is full of fun and genuine wit, but when the words are allowed to particularize the general humor of the setting, the cycle truly sparkles. Ultimately the reason for its success may be stated in a phrase culled from the article on Auric in the 1954 edition of Grove's *Dictionary of Music and Musicians*, but equally applicable to the works of Radiguet: they are "delightfully frivolous but artistically solid."

Notes to Chapter X

1. Charles Koecklin, "Mélodie." *Cinquante ans de Musique française (1874-1925),* edited by L. Rohozinski, p. 1.

2. Jean-Paul Sartre, *Mallarmé or the Poet of Nothingness,* translated by Ernest Sturm (Pennsylvania State University Press, 1988) p. 22:

3. Ibid., p. 24.

4. Ibid., Introduction, p. 7.

5. James McNab, *Raymond Radiguet* (Boston: Twayne Pub., 1984) p. 112.

6. Roger Shattuck, *The Banquet Years* (New York: Harcourt Brace, 1958) p. 18.

7. Jean Cocteau. article written in 1919 in his revue, *Le Coq et l'Arlequin* and dedicated to Auric. Quoted by McNab, p. 18.

8. Shattuck, p. 121 (note)

9. Article on Satie in Grove's *Dictionary of Music and Musicians*, Vol. VII, Fifth Edition (St. Martin's Press. 1954) p. 417.

10. *La Nouvelle Revue française*, February, 1921, pp.224-227.

11. Georges Auric, *Quand j'étais là* (Paris: Grasset, 1979) p.52.

12. Shattuck, p. 29.

13. McNab, p. 14.

14. Auric, p. 22.

15. Ibid., p. 145.

16. McNab, p. 134.

17. Sartre, p. 16.

18. Koecklin, p. 57.

19. Jean-Louis Major, *Radiguet, Cocteau: Les Joues en Feu* (University of Ottawa Press, 1977) p. 24.

20. Ibid.

21. David Noakes, critique of *Alphabet* in *Le Larousse mensuel* of January 1925), p. 13, note 1.

22. Koecklin, p. 57.
23. Auric, p. 39.
24. Noakes, p. 101.

Chapter XI

AARON COPLAND

TWELVE POEMS OF EMILY DICKINSON

Emily Dickinson was born in 1830 in Amherst, Massachusetts, and, aside from a few brief journeys to visit friends or consult doctors, she never left home. Her excellent formal education began at Amherst Academy and continued at the nearby Mount Holyoke Female Seminary; her principal occupation when not writing poetry was caring for her father and mother in their comfortable Amherst home. Neither she nor her sister Lavinia married, and her brother Austin lived with his wife and children in the house next door. She corresponded with several people, but actually saw few, especially after 1862, when serious eye problems threatened her with blindness. Her one certifiable romantic interest—certifiable because both she and the eminent lawyer with whom she fell in love when she was over forty years old acknowledged their feelings in speech and in letters—did not result in marriage even though both seemed to want it. Whether their passion was consummated is not known.

Even more explicitly documented than her late-blooming erotic attachment is Dickinson's complex relationship to God.[1] In 1850 there was a fervent "conversion" movement in Amherst. Most of Dickinson's family and friends eventually claimed to have been individually and personally "enlightened" by faith in a just and omnipotent God, a faith far exceeding the commonly held belief in the existence of God as the Divine Planner. In Dickinson's Congregationalist world of the early 1800's, "proof by Design," the idea that nature and man were too intricately fashioned to have developed without some Divine Architect, was accepted as rational and incontrovertible. To the devout Congregationalist, the very irrefutability of this proof made belief in God inevitable, and hence no sign of merit or Grace. If, on the other hand, one could experience a "conversion," whereby, in a Jonathan Edwards-like "leap of faith," the unprovable attributes of goodness and omnipotence could be granted to God despite the injustices and woes of the world, one was "enlightened." This kind of faith, more Baptist than Congregationalist in its foundations, and far more difficult to sustain because it could not be logically supported, had to be actively sought; once embraced it had to be guarded and renewed regularly. It could never be taken for granted.

Although there was no overt pressure on Dickinson to experience conversion, the very atmosphere she breathed seemed to demand it. The most brilliant minds she encountered at Mount Holyoke Female Seminary, her own coldly legalistic father, and almost everyone else she knew and respected claimed to have felt it and to be far happier for having done so. Nevertheless she refused, regarding what the others saw as 'enlightenment' to be a form of blindness attained only by relinquishing one's independent ability to reason, a view held by her contemporary Ralph Waldo Emerson. This Emily was not prepared to do.

Never for a moment doubting His power, and sometimes even grateful for the vague promise of life after death His existence implied, Dickinson often seemed to regard God as an Enemy. God wooed with promises of immortality, but Death was everyman's lot; His voice was seductive, but to be the bride of Christ was to be the bride of Death, to Dickinson a grotesquely macabre concept. Like a cowardly bully, He used His ultimate weapon—the dread of the unknown that follows Death—to frighten mankind into submission, but she for one would not be cowed into the blind faith of conversion.

Dickinson's views of God, nature, eternity, life and death were constantly shifting, and these swings of mood and attitude are reflected in her poems. Since she never dated a poem and since fewer than twenty of her works were published during her lifetime, establishing a chronology for the 1775 lyrics she left behind was a formidable task. It was accomplished with considerable authority by Thomas H. Johnson in 1955, that is about five years after Copland composed his twelve Dickinson settings. The basis for Johnson's chronology, always somewhat tentative except when a poem is included in a dated letter, revolves around references to external events and changes in Dickinson's difficult and distinctive handwriting.

While quite well-read, Copland was no scholar, and such arcane matters as the chronology of Dickinson's works mattered little if at all to him. To more serious students of her verse, even an approximate idea of the time in which a Dickinson poem was composed can prove enlightening when attempts are being made to ferret out its often elliptical, sometimes ineffable meaning. In any case, the dates and numbers used in the following analyses are Johnson's.

Aaron Copland's own description of the genesis of the *Twelve Poems of Emily Dickinson* is so revealing that we quote from it at length:

> I had not composed for voice and piano since 1928... perhaps because I did not come into contact with suitable texts...Then, while looking through an anthology, I came upon a poem by Emily Dickinson that appealed to me. There was something about her personality and use of language that was fresh, precise, utterly unique—and very American...
>
> I fell in love with one poem, "The Chariot." Its first lines absolutely threw me: "Because I could not stop for Death, he kindly stopped for me; the carriage held but just ourselves and immortality." The idea of this completely unknown girl in Massachusetts seeing herself riding off into immortality with death himself seemed like such an incredible idea! I was very struck by that, especially since it turned out to be true. After I set that poem, I continued reading Emily Dickinson. The more I read, the more her vulnerability and loneliness touched me. I found another poem to set, then one more, and yet another. They accumulated gradually, and when I had perhaps more than six, I began to think about how I would order them. But when I had twelve, they all seemed to run to their right places.

The composer's more formal statement, published as a preface to the Boosey & Hawkes edition of the *Twelve Poems of Emily Dickinson* (more often referred to as "The Emily Dickinson Songs") reads as follows:

These twelve songs were composed at Sneeden's Landing, New York, at various times during the period from March 1949 to March 1950. They are the first works the composer has written for solo voice since 1928. The poems center about no single theme, but they treat of subject matter particularly close to Miss Dickinson: nature, death, life, eternity. Only two of the songs are related thematically, the seventh and the twelfth. Nevertheless, the composer hopes that, in seeking a musical counterpart for the unique personality of the poet, he has given the songs, taken together, the aspect of a song cycle. The twelve songs are dedicated to twelve composer friends.

On the same prefatory page is the statement that the texts Copland used were taken from the edition of Emily Dickinson's poems edited by Martha Dickinson Bianchi and Alfred Leete Hampson. This edition, the result of long years of work (1914-1930), was published by Little, Brown and Company. It restored some of the original spellings, punctuation marks and actual words which had been changed by Mabel Loomis Todd (the mistress of Emily's brother Austin) and Thomas Wentworth Higginson (a well-known critic and writer with whom Emily corresponded about her poetry and on whom she seemed to rely "to say if my Verse is alive"[3] in their *Emily Dickinson Poems, First & Second Series.* Their work was originally published in 1890, just four years after the poet's death. Some of the substitutions in the earlier edition were an attempt to make Dickinson's quirky, enigmatic poetry more comprehensible, more "correct"; others were simply mistaken readings of Dickinson's idiosyncratic handwriting. According to Vivian Perlis, the Yale University historian who specializes in American music and whose collaboration with Copland resulted in a unique two-volume, joint-effort "autobiography," the Bianchi-Hampson edition of Dickinson's poems is not to be found in Copland's library. In its stead is a 1948 reissue of the 1890 volume described above. Obviously Copland consulted both.[4]

Copland was born in Brooklyn, New York, on November 14, 1900. His first ventures into Manhattan were in pursuit of a musical education, and, in 1921, that same quest led him to

Fontainebleau, France where he and Nadia Boulanger discovered one another. He lived in France for two years, making fairly lengthy side-trips to Germany and Italy while he was abroad, and he visited Mexico and South America dozens of times. His aim in these peregrinations was always musical—to find unknown or little-known composers, to hear unfamiliar ethnic rhythms and instruments, to watch folk dances and listen to folk songs, to conduct new American works abroad, and to bring new Latin American compositions home to the States. Along the way, with his equable disposition, he could hardly help meeting lots of people. Hence, although there are few who can claim to have known Copland intimately (his private life has always been just that—private, and titillating gossip finds no place in his autobiography) the number of people who regard themselves as his friends is astounding.

What an amazing contrast all this activity, all this sociability, all this presence in the world, is to the life of Emily Dickinson, the poet with whom Copland felt the closest affinity.

Each of the twelve Dickinson poems chosen by Copland and each of his settings for them can stand as a complete entity, and yet, to quote the composer once again, "I prefer them to be sung as a cycle. They seem to have a cumulative effect."[5] Assuming that the composer knows best, we shall discuss the songs as a continuous group, stopping along the way to subject the first, second, ninth and final songs to particularly detailed examination.

NATURE THE GENTLEST MOTHER

> Nature the gentlest mother
> Impatient of no child
> The feeblest or the waywardest
> Her admonition mild
>
> In forest and the hill
> By traveller is heard
> Restraining rampant squirrel
> or too impetuous bird.

How fair her conversation
A summer afternoon.
Her household, her assembly
And when the sun goes down

Her voice among the aisles
Incites the timid prayer
Of the minutest cricket
The most unworthy flower.

When all the children sleep,
She turns as long away,
As will suffice to light her lamps
Then, bending from the sky,

With infinite affection
And infiniter care
Her golden finger on her lip
Wills silence ev'rywhere.

This rather long poem (written around 1863 and #790 of the 1775 Dickinson is known to have composed) paints Nature in famil3iar rather than transcendental terms. (By 1863, with Thoreau's death the previous year and Emerson's literary career largely behind him, Transcendentalism in American poetry was gradually yielding to Whitmanesque realism. Dickinson may be regarded as a transitional figure.) Its picture of a benign, motherly Nature, whose mild admonitions to her lesser creatures can be overheard by man, the "traveller," is contradicted in many other Dickinson lyrics, but in this poem there is nothing to disturb the peace and tranquility. It is summer and the weather is as non-threatening as Nature's warnings. With perhaps just a touch of the coyness that sometimes accompanies it, Dickinson uses deliberately "domestic" language ("her household," "lights her lamps") and humanizing gestures ("bending from the sky," "her golden finger on her lip") to bring Nature closer to man in scope and stature. Since Dickinson often equated birds and poets, she may be gently reprimanding her own impetuosity, for neither she nor the rampant squirrel has Nature's patience, but she doesn't appear to be too stringent in this self-criticism.

At the beginning of the fourth stanza, with the single word "aisles," Dickinson simply and vividly brings the reader to a variant image, that of Nature both within and as the Church which "Incites the timid prayer." The original trope of Nature as Mother returns, however, in the next line, reinforcing the validity of the poet's childlike use of "waywardest" and "infiniter."

There are three conventionally realized rhymes in this poem (child-mild, heard-bird, care-ev'rywhere) but even in this quasi-traditional evocation of Nature as Mother of all living things, Dickinson favors a more subtle and more idiosyncratic allusion to rhyme in such pairings as hill-squirrel, afternoon-down, prayer-flower and away-sky. The rhythm of the first and third lines, with their heavily stressed trochees, iambs and anapests ("Náture, the géntlest Móther" and "The féeblest and the wáywardest") is probably intended to represent Mother Nature cradling her children to sleep, but Dickinson does not insist on this rocking movement. The two accented syllables at the beginning of the last line, "Wills silence ev'rywhere," seem to stop all motion: the world is asleep now, and it is a sleep born of peace and security.

Copland sets the mood for the song and for the cycle as a whole with an eight-bar piano introduction in which certain musical tropes are established. The movement is to be slow, the sound "crystal-line," as two brief groups of unaccompanied 32nd notes, each ending in a long, sustained B flat (the principal tonality of the piece), begin the music with what might be interpreted as bird-like calls (Ex. I). The opening figure, begun on the last eighth-note of a long 4/4 measure, interrupts a silence evoked by the eighth-note rest which precedes it and the long note on which it ends. (It is crucial for the performers to establish this matrix of silence as part of the music.) Copland had used this device—short groups of rapid notes surrounded either by silence or by single held notes—to similar effect in the middle movement of his Piano Sonata which was composed a decade earlier (Ex II). In the ostensibly non-programmatic Sonata, as in this little prélude, an aural equivalent of the wide-open spaces of the American prairie is created. It is one of those inexplicable phenomena that the image of nineteenth-century America's vast, underpopulated mid-West was so well captured by city-born, city-bred Aaron Copland.

Ex. I

Ex. II

Although the three-flat key signature of this first song should introduce E flat or C minor as the principal tonality, the F,D,B-flat triad at the end of each of the two opening figures as well as the repeated emphasis on B flat itself throughout the introduction clearly overrides the initial indication. One could argue for the importance of B flat as the dominant of E flat, and the final chord does include an E flat within the B flat triad, but nowhere does E flat take command, and Copland's choice of key signature remains puzzling.

In the second measure of the piano prélude, Copland introduces a simple melody, simply, harmonized. Despite—or perhaps because of—its lack of intricacy, the two-bar secion, essentially in two-part harmony, is delicate and elegant. Here too the emphasis is strongly on the key of B flat. Sustained notes at the beginnings of the next three bars reinforce the wide-open-space atmosphere, and an intensified reiteration of the 32nd-note figure, now made even more bird-like by the grace-notes adorning the high C's and ending on the longest, most widely-spaced B flats to date, prepare for the singer's entrance.

Copland sets the first line of the poem with utmost simplicity. Sung on just two notes, D and B flat, the melodic phrases follow

the gently rocking speech cadences of the words, while the piano
part creates a mildly polyrhythmic pattern of its own. Until the
second word of the second line ("of") there is no tone outside the
B flat triad. At "of no child," we finally move to an E flat triad,
but the B flat bass note is sustained. As befits the word "waywardest," the tempo of real and harmonic motion picks up for a
while, but Dickinson's "mild" pulls the music back for a sustained
F minor triad.

Copland continues to underscore almost every important word
in the poem with an appropriate musical gesture, moving forward
in both tempo and rate of harmonic motion—the latter by way of
an unexpected D flat in the melodic line and an equally surprising
D flat chord in the accompaniment—at "traveller." He creates a
bit of dissonance as well as busier figurations for "rampant
squirrel" and "impetuous bird," and composes a nice chatty
dialogue for the piano's upper and lower lines at "How fair her
conversation." Making no attempt at a church-like setting for the
first two lines of the fourth stanza, however, Copland instead
chooses to build to a busy, noisy climax, ending the section in a
loud, discordant trill after "The most unworthy flower." This
jangling piano interlude gradually fades, yielding to yet another
widely-spaced (there are four octaves between the two notes) B flat
unison, after which the singer continues in the slower tempo of the
beginning with "When all the children sleep."

The melodic line for "Bending from the sky" does just that—it
bends way down from the E flat a tenth above middle C to the E
flat an octave below and then straightens up to the C above. The
birds are not yet all asleep, as three little 32nd-note figures in the
accompaniment attest, but gradually all grows still. The even,
sustained half-notes Copland allots to each syllable in his first
statement of the last line of text obviates Dickinson's
strong/strong/weak/strong/weak/strong rhythm (Wílls sí lence év
'ry whére), creating instead a moment of beatless, hence motionless, enchantment. At his repeat of this verse Copland actually
contradicts the poet's stress-pattern, emphasizing the two unaccented syllables by making each of them three beats long while leaving
the other syllables as half-notes. The exquisite effect of these final
lines, made all the more compelling by the beauty of the singer's
low B flat under the piano's final chord, with its last, sleepy,

bird-call double grace-note and its subtle hint of E flat within the
B flat triad, makes it hard to criticize the composer for taking these
liberties with the text.

As though to emphasize Dickinson's shifting and apparently
contradictory attitude toward Nature (as one of her biographers
said of the poet, "She did not possess a talent for conviction"[6]
Copland chooses to follow her "gentlest Mother" image with
"There came a wind like a bugle," a picture of Nature at her most
rambunctious (#1593, written in 1883).

THERE CAME A WIND LIKE A BUGLE

> There came a wind like a bugle,
> It quivered through the grass,
> And a green chill upon the heat
> so ominous did pass.
>
> We barred the window and the doors
> As from an emerald ghost
> The doom's electric moccasin
> that very instant passed.
>
> On a strange mob of panting trees
> and fences fled away
> And rivers where the houses ran
> the living looked that day.
>
> The bell within the steeple wild
> The flying tidings whirled
> How much can come And much can go
> And yet abide the world.

According to Cynthia Griffin Wolff, Dickinson saw the basic
pattern of English hymnody, alternating lines of eight and six
syllables or "eights and sixes" as they were called, as an attribute
she must combat in her ongoing struggle against God's seductive-
ness, and hence "as a model to strain against and violate."[7] Many
poems may be cited to support this hypothesis, but "There came a
wind like a bugle" is not one of them, for here the "eights and

sixes" are perfect and unvarying.

Where Dickinson does seem to fight the hymnal norm is in the variety of metrical feet she employs. Most of the lines are indeed in standard, English speech-pattern iambs, but the complex mixture of beats in the powerful opening verses of the first and third strophes as well as in line three of the initial quatrain shows Dickinson's independence.

Perhaps Dickinson felt free to use the "eights and sixes" pattern so familiar to all New England Congregationalist churchgoers just because the scene this particular poem paints is so remote from religious concerns. The subject is, quite obviously, a storm, an electric storm in summer, which resulted in rivers flooded enough to carry houses away right in front of one's eyes. However clear the general outline, we should not be surprised that some of the imagery is nevertheless far from obvious, for Dickinson saw poetry as "a complex game of hide-and-seek that a poet may play with her reader..." (Wolff, op cit, p 128). "Green chill" is a wonderful metaphor for the wind blowing through the summer grass, made even more remarkable by its implied equation with an "emerald ghost" in the following stanza and the still stronger "doom's electric moccasin" in the next line. (Perhaps a little esoteric for today's city dwellers, the definition of "moccasin" as a poisonous snake would have been more familiar in Dickinson's time.) This bugle-like wind takes the breath away from the very trees and fences, leaving them "panting" as it finally flies away.

The entire poem bristles with motion and energy: the bell goes wild in the steeple, whirling its "flying tidings," and objects as solid as houses, which we normally think of as fixed and immobile, run on the rivers. Only the last two lines, with their slow-moving, single-syllable, deliberately nonevocative words, stem the rushing meter and metaphors. "Abide," the only word with more than one syllable in the last two lines, has such rich connotations of religious and secular stability that its inclusion reinforces the cessation of motion accomplished by the extreme simplicity of the other terms chosen by the poet for the ending of the poem.

Copland has the piano begin the song with a musical metaphor for the brassy wind—explosively rushing rising scales, played a dissonant ninth apart by the two hands, ending on a D major chord

(Ex I). The singer makes her first statement in free recitative style over the held harmony, but after the two-note rising phrase for "bugle" a cacaphonous piano figure rushes in to carry the vocal part along on its wildly energetic course (Ex II).

Ex I

Ex II

The word "ghost," sung on an unexpected high E sharp, precipitates a "scared" downward tumble in the accompaniment, while dissonances and a long trill contribute to the exhilarating energy of the musical scenario. Copland has the piano part anticipate the bell wildly ringing in the steeple, beginning the left hand's eighth-note/quarter note, eighth-note/quarter note pattern and the right hand's clangorous sixteenth-note figure almost two measures before the singer gives voice to Dickinson's image. The vocal line here consists of even eighth-notes, but the composer's eccentric melodic motion and phrasing effectively convey the irregular ringing of a wildly oscillating bell.

Clashing rising scales like those at the beginning of the song, but now at an interval of a major seventh and resulting in a mildly dissonant F# minor seventh chord (E, F#, A, C#) imitate the bugle-like wind one last time before the song's finale. Copland's instruction to the performers at "How much can come" is "Broadly, forte, with emphasis." Evidently he does not hear the last two lines as peacefully philosophic so much as boldly triumphant. He

insists on dissonance right up to the end: the singer's final low C#
is sung to a consonant A chord (the tonality of the piece is A
major) but this is immediately followed by what amounts to a tone
cluster consisting of D#, F#, E and B in the accompaniment; this
pattern is repeated once and then, in the penultimate measure,
softened so that only the F# remains to spice the final A major
chord.   As the low A fades, only the combination of E and F#
above middle C "abides."

A single loud, accented four-note unison on C (actually three
whole notes and an introductory grace note) startles the listener
into readiness for Dickinson's next text, "Why do they shut me out
of Heaven?" (#248, written in 1861).

WHY DO THEY SHUT ME OUT OF HEAVEN

> Why do they shut me out of Heaven?
> Did I sing too loud?
> But I can sing a little minor,
> Timid as a bird.
>
> Wouldn't the angels
> try me just once more
> Just see if I troubled them
> But don't shut the door
> [don't shut the door.]
>
> Oh if I were the gentlemen
> in the white robes
> and they were the little hand that knocked,
> Could I forbid? [Could I forbid? Could I forbid?]
>
> [Why do they shut me out of Heaven?
> Did I sing too loud?]

The three phrases of text repeated in the song by Copland—
"don't shut the door," "Could I forbid?" and the first two lines as
used at the end—are shown here in brackets.   There is one other
fairly significant variant, found in the third line, which is quoted
in the collected poems as "But I can say a little 'Minor,'" which
to those educated in philosophy, as Dickinson was, might suggest

major and minor premises as well as musical modes, especially
since Dickinson puts the word "minor" in quotation marks.

Without the repeated phrases the poem is of course considerably
shorter, but—more important for the composer—its rhythms are
also much quirkier, with the last line, a mere four syllables, the
shortest segment of the text. In the first and third stanzas long and
short lines alternate, but with only a remote reference to the
"eights and sixes" of Congregationalist hymnody. The middle
stanza abandons even this loose scheme, with line three seven
syllables long and the others five syllables each. "Loud" and
"bird," the ends of lines two and four, qualify as a suggestion of
rhyme in Dickinson's works, and "more" and "door" of the next
stanza constitute a true enough rhyme, but there is no attempt at
similar end sounds for the final stanza. It is clear to see that
ending a song with the abrupt and unrhymed "Could I forbid?"
would be almost impossible, and Copland may be forgiven for
repeating the opening couplet.

While obviously aware of the poignancy lying behind it,
Copland emphasizes the humorous nature of the poem. This is
most apparent in the settings of the word "loud," where the singer
has loud, high, strident notes, arrived at by leaps—first from the
C flat one octave above middle C to the G flat a fifth above, and
then from the same C flat to the even higher A flat. "Timid as a
bird" is charmingly set, with even staccato 16th notes in more or
less contrary motion for piano and voice (Ex I). One appreciates
the charm even more if one remembers that for Dickinson the bird
was often a metaphor for the poet, and for herself in particular.

Ex I

The next song, "The World feels dusty," (#715) and written
around 1863, is a setting of one of Dickinson's many poems
dealing with death.

THE WORLD FEELS DUSTY

> The world feels dusty
> When we stop to die
> We want the dew then
> Honors taste dry.
>
> Flags vex a dying face
> But the least fan
> Stirred by a friend's hand
> Cools like the rain.
>
> Mine be the ministry
> when thy thirst comes
> Dews of thyself to fetch
> and holy balms.

Like all women of her generation, Emily Dickinson was all-too-well acquainted with death. It was the job of nineteenth-century New England women to nurse the sick and to keep watch over the dying, and even pre-adolescent girls were pressed into service when illness struck. Even in Dickinson's limited acquaintanceship, so many young people died of consumption, so many children died of fevers, so many women died during or soon after childbirth, that death could not be associated exclusively, or even primarily, with the old or the singularly unfortunate. Moreover, the poem was written in the midst of the Civil War when Amherst and the other small Massachusetts towns received almost weekly their reports of young men dying in battle.

No matter how familiar death seemed, however, its true meaning was forever beyond the realm of human experience. There were three choices for the poet—to maintain an awed silence in the face of its mystery, to infuse it with meaning by invoking the symbols of religion, or to domesticate it by speaking of it in ordinary, homespun language. Quite obviously, and in several of her best-known poems, Dickinson chose the third course. Only in the last two lines of this example does the poetic construction present some difficulty in the otherwise straightforward text ("Dews of thyself to fetch"); the reading that most readily presents itself is that genuine solace, or "dews," although ministered by the protagonist, will actually have emanated from the dying person, from his or her own attributes.

In this song Copland respects the integrity of the text, setting each syllable with its own melodic note, repeating nothing, altering nothing. Slow, stately chords introduce and support the vocal line for the first six bars, after which eighth-notes on the final beats of the next two measures help create some forward motion. All the key words—"dry," "rain" and "balm," are sung on low pitches, as though to emphasize the gravity of the statements. The highest note occurs on the word "Flags," and the line beginning with that word exhibits the most energy. The chords of the piano postlude create a symmetrical frame with those in the two-bar prelude. There is remarkable simplicity of both the text and its setting in this brief jewel of a song.

The fifth of the Copland-Dickinson songs, "Heart, we will forget him," might masquerade as a popular romantic ballad if American pop-music tastes were more sophisticated. Its text, #47, written around 1858, is of the genre that has led biographers to postulate a thwarted love interest in the poet's life prior to the acknowledged one of her later years.

HEART, WE WILL FORGET HIM

> Heart, we will forget him
> You and I, tonight.
> You may forget the warmth he gave
> I will forget the light.
>
> When you have done, pray tell me,
> That I my thoughts may dim
> Haste lest while you're lagging
> I may remember him.

Copland states that critics have found influences of Ives, Fauré and Mahler in his Dickinson songs, in particular linking Mahler with "Heart, we will forget him,"[9] but that he sees no direct influences. This commentator is inclined to agree with the composer, at least as regards this song, unless one wishes to

attribute Copland's use of almost constant modulation in it to the
influence of the Austrian post-Romantic school, of which Mahler
was a star exponent. There are two particularly beautiful modulations in the song—one at "tonight" (Ex I) and one at "the light"
(Ex. II); the establishment of the pure E flat chord in the last three
measures is made all the more effective and affecting because of
the intricate chord relationships that precede it. Because throughout the first five songs Copland has so consistently set the words
syllabically, i.e., one note per syllable and one syllable per note,
the two-note phrases on "warmth" and "him" are particularly
telling.

Ex. I

Ex. II

With the sixth song, "Dear March, come in!" (#1320, c. 1874)
we return to Dickinson's nature poetry.

DEAR MARCH, COME IN

> Dear March, come in How glad I am
> I looked for you before.
> Put down your hat You must have walked
> How out of breath you are.

Dear March, how are you? And the rest?
Did you leave Nature well?
Oh, March come right upstairs with me
I have so much to tell.

I got your letter and the bird's
The maples never knew
that you were coming, I declare
How red their faces grew,

But March, forgive me. And all those hills
you left for me to hue,
There was no purple suitable,
You took it all with you.

Who knocks? that April? Lock the door,
I will not be pursued
He stayed away a year to call
when I am occupied

But trifles look so trivial
As soon as you have come
And blame is just as dear as praise
And praise as mere as blame.

According to R. B. Sewall, the months of the year had definite
personalities for Dickinson, and March, about which she wrote five
poems, was her favorite. This should not be surprising, for March
signals the beginning of the end of the long New England winter,
the month when the sap begins to run in the maple trees and the
days' lengthening becomes a significant factor against the cold
winds and snowstorms yet to come. As Dickinson herself said,

Without the Snow's Tableau
Winter were lie—to me—
Because I see New Englandly[11]

There are many personal notes in the text: from Dickinson, who became more and more of a recluse as the years went by, an invitation to "come right upstairs" to her private rooms was a rarity indeed, proferred seldom if ever to any but the closest members of the family. She speaks of herself as left behind the year before to "hue" the hills, but without the "purple suitable" to the task. If this is a reference to her declining powers (this is a relatively late poem and she did write less in her later years) the thought is belied by the energy and forceful voice of the poem itself, perhaps a sign that, after a fallow period, the coming of March had once again rekindled her own poetic spark.

In general Dickinson did not seem to share the Emersonian/ Wordsworthian view that man and nature might have a benign reciprocal relationship, but in this chatty poem March and Nature are personified, and they and the poet share an intimacy in which loving friendship and petulant annoyance (April's knocking after a whole year's absence is viewed as impertinent) are mingled. The last two lines have the ring of a "sticks and stones may break my bones" aphorism, one used by children to taunt one another or perhaps by adults as a moral lesson. They seem remarkably quaint and prim after the wild exuberance of the rest of the poem.

  Once again, perhaps since the poem is devoid of religious associations, Dickinson feels free to use the "eights and sixes" which seem to come naturally to her, deviating from the strict count in only one line—"Dear March, forgive me. And all those hills," which has nine syllables. Half of the B/D lines are fully rhymed, half are merely suggestive of rhyme. Since it would not have been difficult to juggle the "come"-"blame" combination to "came"-"blame," we must surmise that these idiosyncratic assonances are deliberate replacements for the more ordinary full rhymes. As such they may be taken as examples of Dickinson's insistent independence from poetic convention.

Copland matches the vigor of Dickinson's poem in his brilliant setting. From the opening two-bar piano prelude, the composer's simultaneous use of the six-sharp key-signature's major and relative minor, F# and D# respectively, is boldly exposed, its effect heightened by the held pedal indicated in the score. This

same polytonal harmony, "delicately" rolled (we quote the composer's instruction), constitutes the last chord of the song; it is one
of Copland's favorite polytonal devices, essential to the main
theme of the first movement of the Piano Sonata, for example, and
found in many other of his compositions.

The piano's introductory figure, with its clanging, rollicking 6/8
meter (Ex I), is the characteristic sound of blustery March
throughout the song. There is a momentary clash between the two
parts when the piano plays a C major chord under the singer's C#
at the end of the first vocal phrase, but this harsh dissonance
immediately yields to a consonance as the piano moves to an F#
chord under the vocalist's held C# (Ex. II). This pattern is
repeated for "Dear March, how are you?", and a similar disso-
nance-consonance shift underscores "And the rest?"

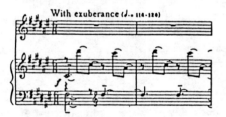

Ex. I

Ex. II

There is less clatter under the conversational "I got your letter,"
but the sound level gradually grows again until a climax is reached
on a big C major chord at "How red their faces grew." The piano
is silent as the voice expresses its surprise and dismay at April's
arrival, but noisy, agitated intervals of a second in the characteristic rocking rhythm bring the accompaniment back to its original
high-energy level. The music becomes suitably calmer for the

aphoristic last lines, and widely spaced polytonal chords (the
by-now familiar F#-D# minor, but here spiced with a G#), played
"indifferently" according to the composer's instructions, surround
the singer's final low D# (which is held for five long measures),
before everything melts into the last soothing chord.

With a canny ear for contrast, Copland chooses an introspective
Dickinson poem to follow "Dear March, come in!" Its opening
line (few of Dickinson's poems have titles, so all are catalogued
according to first lines) is "Sleep is supposed to be," and it was
found in a letter written to her father in 1858. The letter reads in
part "To my Father- to whose untiring efforts in my behalf, I am
indebted for my morning hours, viz.—3 A.M. to 12 P.M.—these
grateful lines are inscribed by his Affectionate Daughter."

SLEEP IS SUPPOSED TO BE

> Sleep is supposed to be,
> By souls of sanity,
> The shutting of the eye
>
> Sleep is the station grand
> Down which on either hand
> The hosts of witness stand
>
> Morn is supposed to be,
> By people of degree,
> The breaking of the day,
>
> Morning has not occurred
> That shall aurora be
> East of Eternity
>
> One with the banner gay
> One in the red array
> That is the break of day.

One of Dickinson's many intriguingly enigmatic poems, "Sleep
is supposed to be" seems to beg for an interpretation exposing
profundities only hinted at in the actual words. A freely-associa-

tive paraphrase might read: Sane people (are they alive or dead?—"souls" can imply either) suppose that sleep (is Dickinson using sleep as the usual metaphor for death?) is the closing of the eye (according to Cynthia Griffin Wolff, "eye" equals "I" for Dickinson, hence the shutting of the eye equals the closing up of the I, another way of describing death). Sleep is the large and impressive place on either side of which stand hosts (hostile armies? neutral multitudes? guests? those who receive guests? animals or organisms in or on whose organs parasites exist? animals used as sacrifices? consecrated wafers representing the body of Christ and individually consumed in a Protestant communion in mid-nineteenth century Amherst by Congregationalists who had experienced "conversion"?—the dictionary lists all these meanings and Dickinson would have known them all). People who are assumed to know, by dint of their standing in the community (pedigree) or higher education, or perhaps because they are already dead souls (but then shouldn't they be certain?) suppose that Morning (if heard but not seen, indistinguishable from Mourning) is the breaking (beginning or destruction?) of the day. The Garden of Eden lies East of Eternity and the dawn, that brilliant display that greets us as we awaken at break of day, has yet to occur there. Does this imply that the dead, contrary to orthodox religious thought, do not reawaken in the hereafter and that Earth is hence preferable to Eden; a humanistic view which was put forth in various forms by both the Unitarians and Universalists of New England?

The unusual number of major triads reminiscent of church music in Copland's setting of "Sleep is supposed to be" clearly reflects the religious allusions in Dickinson's text. The jarring note of the poet's disturbing question, which might be inferred from the poem, is also reproduced in musical terms by the composer, for the sharp dissonance of C against C flat occurs several times in the music. Appropriately enough, the first time is before the singer's forte entrance at "Morning has not occurred," the beginning of the suggestion of painful doubt.

Copland says that "although the [Dickinson] songs are commonly referred to as a 'cycle,' only two are related musically—the seventh ["Sleep is"] and twelfth ["The Chariot"]."[13] These texts are also related in subject matter, both falling under the

heading of what one Dickinson biographer calls "proleptic poems,".[14] i.e. those speaking of the hereafter as though the poet has
knowledge of thereof "Morning has not occurred/ that shall aurora
be/ East of Eternity"). Still talking about his Dickinson Songs,
Copland also states that he has "always had an aversion to
repeating myself.[15] Nevertheless strong resemblances between the
opening bars of "Sleep is supposed to be" (Ex I) and the main
theme of the third movement of the Piano Sonata, composed a
decade earlier (Ex II), cannot be denied.

Ex. I

Ex. II

The text for the eighth song, "When they come back," is a
syntactically strange combination of incomplete statements and
long, explanatory asides. There are no overt religious overtones
to its obvious preoccupation with death, and its references to
blossoms, robins, and May, as well as its jauntily vernacular last
line, give it a lightheartedness quite at variance with the seriousness of the doubts it expresses. One wonders how literally to take
Dickinson's "tomorrow"—is it the tomorrow that never comes?
She and the reader know that, even if the Spring she lovingly
describes should return every year throughout eternity, at some
future "tomorrow" she as an individual will not be "there" to "take
back all I say," unless the "there" she envisions is some kind of
reincarnation into Nature itself, a thought not usually associated

with her poetry. The meter of "When they come back" is in regular "eights and sixes" and its B/D end-sounds display the usual Dickinsonian mixture of true rhyme, suggestion of rhyme, and no rhyme at all.

WHEN THEY COME BACK

When they come back if blossoms do,
I always feel a doubt
If blossoms can be born again
When once the art is out.

When they begin if robins do
I always had a fear
I did not tell it was their last
Experiment last year.

When it is May, if May return,
Has nobody a pang
that on a face so beautiful
we might not look again.

If I am there, one does not know
what party one may be
tomorrow, But if I am there,
I take back all I say!

Copland's setting for "When they come back" begins in a spirit reminiscent of that of the first Dickinson song, "Nature, the gentlest Mother." For three measures the piano's quietly expressive eighth-notes pass through lovely shifting harmonies, settling on an F major chord as introduction to and support of the singer's first phrase, which is also an F major triad. Since this opening phrase, "When they come back," ends with a downward interval to the tonic of the F major chord, it has the aura of a positive statement, but the next four syllables, "if blossoms do," sung as they are on a rising E flat triad, imply a question. As the singer elaborates the poet's doubts, the music grows faster and more agitated. Dissonance initiated under "I always had a fear" increases, culminating in a climactic fortissimo at the word "year," which is sung on a high F# after a leap of a ninth from the E natural more than an octave below. Clangorous effects following this peak and continuing at "When it is May" remind the listener of the picture of nature gone wild which Dickinson and Copland have already painted in "There came a Wind like a Bugle."

The music becomes slower, gentler and more harmonious as the words speak of May's beauty, preparing the listener for the singer's sedate calm at the final stanza. Copland suspends the accompaniment for the curiously pert last line, "I take back all I say," which is sung at the tempo of the beginning but now sounds somewhat faster because of the intervening ritards. There is a brief flare-up of excitement in the piano postlude, but calm prevails as the final F major chord is allowed to fade away.

"I felt a funeral in my brain," #280, c. 1861, the text chosen by Copland for the ninth of the twelve songs, is one of the most frequently anthologized and thoroughly analyzed of all the Dickinson poems. The words in lines three and six, here shown in brackets, were added by the composer for metrical reasons, and one full stanza, the last in the original poem, does not appear in the song.

I FELT A FUNERAL IN MY BRAIN

I felt a funeral in my brain,
And mourners to and fro,
Kept treading, treading, [treading] till it seemed
that sense was breaking through.

And when they all were seated
A service like a drum
Kept beating, beating, [beating] till I thought
my mind was going numb.

And then I heard them lift a box,

And creak across my soul
With those same boots of lead again,
Then space began to toll

As all the heavens were a bell
And Being but an Ear,
And I and silence some strange race
Wrecked solitary here.

The final stanza, which Copland does not include, speaks of the breaking of the "Plank of Reason," the free-thinker's substitute for orthodoxy's "Plank of Faith." This latter was a common icon, pictorially represented in many religious texts as a bridge over the abyss between Life and Heaven. Since man cannot cross this great chasm without some sort of bridge, and since Dickinson says that the only plank she is prepared to accept—that of reason—does not hold up, we must assume that the poet sees herself and/or her protagonist reenacting the original Fall into bottomless chaos.

On April 25, 1862, Dickinson sent "I felt a Funeral" to Thomas Higginson with the following comments: "I had a terror—since September—I could tell to none—and so I sing, as the Boy does by the Burying Ground—because I am afraid."[16] Unlike the Boy's song, however, this poem hardly serves to alleviate terror.

Cynthia Wolff characterizes Dickinson's "voice" when writing of death as "proleptic, Gothic, suffused with transcendent knowledge, essentially and deliberately literary."[17] She sees in the death poems influences of Poe, Byron and the Book of Revelations. Certainly the rhythmic repetitions of "treading" and "beating" (especially as heightened by Copland's further repetitions) and the alliterative "felt a funeral" and "creak across my soul" are reminiscent of Poe's language, and the claustrophobic situation the verses imply of someone imprisoned within a coffin, obviously though inexplicably dead, powerless to react and yet possessed of enough sensory awareness to feel his mind going numb, could easily form the basis for one of his short stories.

Wolff further points out that although the funeral felt in the protagonist's brain follows the pattern of all such New England Congregationalist rites, the feature which should be central to it—the minister's eulogy linking the deceased's past life on earth to his future life in Heaven—is missing. This absence robs the poem of its own basic structural center.[18] "The speaker seems to strain after coherence," says Wolff ("sense" is trying to "break through"), but all is a "disjunctive jumble" because of the "disruptive capacity" of death. The speechless funeral service, a religious ritual devoid of intellectual content, is a drumming, mind-numbing exercise. "Space," the entire atmosphere, begins to echo the tolling bell; the essence of life is hearing, but the dead one is shipwrecked on some indescribable "here" with silence for her/his only companion.

Copland's setting reflects the dimming of the protagonist's consciousness, going from a loud, "rather fast" beginning to a slow, quiet, fade-out ending. The devices the composer uses along the way are fairly obvious ones—a relentlessly pounding march rhythm created by persistent quarter-note chords over a clangorous 16th-note figure in the piano part for the introduction and the first stanza, "thud-like" chords and "exaggerated" accents on the first beats of the measures (both specified by the composer) to indicate the "beating, beating, beating" of the drums, heavily inflected two-note phrases in the melodic line for the "treading, treading, treading," bell-like chords high in the piano's treble clef for the tolling of the bells, and dissonances throughout. The isolation of the last word, "here," separated from the rest of the stanza by a break in the phrase (there is an eighth-note rest between the syllabically stated "solitary" and "here") and from the accompaniment by harmonic function (the F on which the last word is sung has no place in the E flat seven chord over which it floats) reflects the isolation of the protagonist, who has only silence for a ship-wreck mate.

The next text, "I've heard an organ talk sometimes," comes as a charmingly conciliatory statement after the Gothic horror of "I felt a Funeral in my Brain":

I'VE HEARD AN ORGAN TALK SOMETIMES

> I've heard an organ talk sometimes
> In a cathedral aisle
> And understood no word it said.
> Yet held my breath the while

And risen up and gone away
A more Bernardine girl
And know not what was done to me
In that old hallowed aisle.

Dickinson's meaning is clear in this little poem—the wordless
message of the church's aura moves her in some inexplicable,
nonrational way, making her "more Bernardine," that is, more like
the monks of the order of Saint Bernard. Any hint of deep
conviction is subverted by the diminishing "girl," for what girls
think or feel need never be taken too seriously (Dickinson suffered
from her father's unremitting antagonism toward intellectual
women;[19] on more than one occasion she used irony to express her
own views on the subject).

Copland's "gently flowing" setting has a few strong dissonances
to enliven its characteristic, richly resounding, "sonore" chords.
The first occurs in the sixth and last measure of the piano's
introduction, where a sustained D natural clashes with a D flat; a
milder one is heard at the end of the first line of text when the
memory of an A natural in both the vocal and the piano parts
makes the strong A flat of the accompaniment under "sometimes"
seem dissonant. A third—this the strongest—flavors "In a
cathedral" with an accompanying chord consisting of D flat, F and
A flat surrounding the singer's E natural. From this biting moment
on, all is consonance, the music apparently reflecting the singer's
peaceful, passive acceptance of whatever was "done" to her "in
that hallowed aisle."

The wide spacing of so many of the chords, with their root notes
reverberating deep in the bass registers of the piano, suggests the
overtones of a church organ; the long pedals necessitated by having
to sustain chords while continuing with notes out of the hand's
reach (see measures six, seven and eight, and—even more
effective—bars nine, seven, five and three from the end) add to the
echo effect so often encountered when organs play in high-vaulted
cathedrals.

The first four stanzas of the penultimate text, "Going to
Heaven," might be taken as a refutation not only of "Why do they
shut me out of Heaven," but of all the nihilistically trepidatious
proleptic death poems in the Dickinson output, but the fifth stanza

sets the record straight—the poet does not believe a word of what she has been saying. As she stated in another poem,

> "Heaven" is what I cannot reach!
> The Apple on the Tree—
> Provided it do hopeless—hang—
> That—"Heaven" is—to Me!

The last four lines of "Going to Heaven" explain only too poignantly why the poet wishes she could believe what she herself has written in the exuberant beginning.

GOING TO HEAVEN!

> Going to Heaven! [repeated twice] I don't know when
> Pray do not ask me how
> Indeed I'm too astonished
> to think of answering you
>
> Going to Heaven! [repeated twice] How dim it sounds.
> And yet it will be done
> As sure as flocks go home at night
> Unto the shepherd's arm!
>
> Perhaps you're going too! Who knows?
> If you should get there first
> Save just a little place for me,
> Close to the two I lost
>
> The smallest robe will fit me
> and just a bit of "crown"
> for you know we do not mind our dress
> when we are going home.
>
> Going to Heaven! [repeated twice] I'm glad I don't believe
> it
> for it would stop my breath
> And I'd like to look a little more
> at such a curious earth

> I am glad they did believe it
> Whom I have never found
> Since the mighty autumn afternoon
> I left them in the ground.

The tone of the poem, at least until the final stanza, is buoyant, chatty and domestic, expressing joy not at the thought of death itself, but at the idea of Heaven, the site of the glorious afterlife the poet at first seems to envision with such certainty. And what a warm, friendly, homey place this Heaven is made to seem, one in which there is no need for fancy clothes, and lost loved ones will be found again. Curiously enough the tone does not change at all for the stanza in which the poet negates all she has said before—she is glad she does not believe in Heaven, for that belief would kill her and she is not yet tired of life on earth. The last stanza is the most poignant, for the poet acknowledges that without faith in an afterlife for herself, she cannot find "the two" she lost (her parents?); still, she is happy that they believed, although she does not tell us why.

The ambivalence of the entire poem is summarized musically in the last four bars of the setting: Copland ends the vocal line on the E above middle C which the singer is supposed to hold for the entire four bars of the postlude; the piano follows this E with a dissonace strong enough to have been taken from "I felt a Funeral in my Brain" (B, G, A, C#), some of whose harmonies it resembles. In the next measure this discord yields in hymn-like manner to a consonant E major chord, but just as the listener is fairly certain that the song will end on this orthodox sound, a fragment of the piano's characteristic staccato eighth-note figure—a rising line on notes 1,2,3,4,6 of the F major scale—subverts any such complacency. The F-scale fragment is played softly, but the pedal holds everything so that the final sound is never completely clarified.

Copland has the piano begin the song with an attention-getting F, set off by the G a ninth above played as a grace-note. The singer enters with the same scale-fragment described above (Ex. I), after which the accompaniment elaborates on this exuberantly rising figure (Ex. II). The fast 6/8 time, made ever more interesting by unusually placed accents and contrapuntal intricacies

(Ex. III) characterizes the song until the very last stanza, where Copland, like Dickinson, changes the mood. This he does by slowing the tempo, setting the vocalist's syllables to dotted quarter-notes instead of eighth-notes, and using long, sustained chords instead of the bouncy characteristic figure as accompaniment.

Ex. I

Ex. II

Ex. III

The first Dickinson poem to which Copland was attracted, and the first he set to music, was The Chariot (#712, c. 1863), more commonly known by its first line, "Because I could not stop for Death." (The text in the Boosey & Hawkes edition of the songs reads "Because I would not stop for death," but Copland quotes the line correctly when speaking of the poem in his autobiography.) The composer can offer no explanation as to why he decided to save The Chariot for last in the cycle. His instinctive ordering, however, seems not only correct but inevitable, for what could follow this last poem?

THE CHARIOT

Because I could not stop for Death
He kindly stopped for me.
The carriage held but just ourselves
and immortality.

We slowly drove He knew no haste
and I had put away
My labour and my leisure too
For his civility.

We passed the school where children played,
Their lessons scarcely done
We passed the fields of gazing grain
We passed the setting sun,

We paused before a house that seemed
a swelling of the ground
The roof was scarcely visible
the cornice but a mound.

Since then 'tis centuries but each
feels shorter than the day,
I first surmised the horses' heads
were toward eternity.

It is not difficult to see why reading The Chariot should make
one think of Thornton Wilder's 1938 play, "Our Town." In this
Pulitzer-Prize winning piece the namesake of the Amherst,
Massachusetts poet, Emily of Grover's Corners, New Hampshire,
has died bearing her first child. The young woman describes her
own funeral with a peaceful acceptance those left behind on Earth
cannot imagine.

The most striking difference between the two Emilys is their
assessment of their eventual fate: Wilder's protagonist gradually
fades into the mass of humanity that has preceded her; her own
personality and history will be submerged and forgotten when
those few who knew and loved her have gone. Dickinson on the

other hand looks with certainty upon her unique and eternal immortality. It is perhaps this confidence that gives "Because I could not stop for Death" its equanimity, for unlike "I felt a Funeral in my Brain," there is no Gothic horror, no claustrophobic nightmare, in this poem, which was written only two years later.

Cynthia Wolff finds in *The Chariot* a fusion of the "Bride-of-Christ" tradition and the romantic narrative of seduction.[20] In her analysis of the poem, Death is God's emissary, sent to woo the poet with his wiles. Like the villain in the seduction romance, he carries the virgin away with him, but in this Christian version of the story, a bizarrely happy ending is permitted: this despoiled virgin, unlike those who have succumbed to mortal man, need not renounce her lover and give herself to God— God, in the guise of Death, is Himself the false seducer.

Wolff's angry description of the poem, which speaks of the "prurience" of God's role as bridegroom, the "macabre unnaturalness" of any courtship carried on by way of the grave and the "sadism" of an omnipotent Being who claims to woo as a Lover but sends Death in His stead, seems wide of the mark, for the tone of the poem is calm and pleasant. Above all the last stanza, in which the poet, like the other Emily, remarks on the swift passage of time in the life after death, seems proudly contented. More pleasant as well as more appropriate are Denis Donoghue's remarks, according to which Dickinson's poem domesticates grim death, turning him into an Amherst gentleman who has come to call.

As Copland has stated, the setting he wrote for *The Chariot* is related musically to that of the seventh text, "Sleep is supposed to be"; both bear strong resemblances to the elegiac last movement of the composer's Piano Sonata. Example I is the opening of "Sleep is supposed to be," Example II is the introduction to *The Chariot*, and Example III is taken from the Sonata.

The voice participates in the characteristic rhythmic figure shown above to a far greater extent in *The Chariot* than it had in "Sleep is supposed to be," sharing in the sometimes two-part (Ex. IV) sometimes three-part (Ex. V) melodic texture Copland weaves so beautifully with it. At "stopped for me," the singer must negotiate one of those very large intervalic drops—in this case a major ninth—found so often in Copland's works.

Sleep   is   supposed   to   be,............

Ex. I

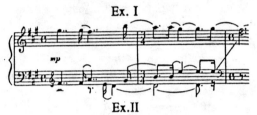

Ex. II

Ex. III

Ex. IV

selves .... and   Im-mor-tal - i - ty........

Ex. V

A new rhythmic figure is introduced in the accompaniment to set off "We slowly drove." This slow-motion horse's gait continues for most of the stanza, after which the original rhythm returns. An arresting modulation underscores the word "sun," and a strong dissonance marks Copland's reaction to the house that seemed "a swelling in the ground." Peaceful yet majestic music sets the last stanza, with a quietly sung, but long sustained, high F# ending the vocal part. Under this held note the original piano figure moves quietly, finally surrounding the singer's last tone with the rest of the B major chord to which it belongs—a most satisfying, fully consonant ending to this remarkable cycle.

Notes to Chapter XII

1. Much of the material dealing with Dickinson's religious beliefs is based on Cynthia Griffin Wolff's *Emily Dickinson* (New York: Knopf, 1986). Since these ideas permeate Ms. Wolff's book, no specific page references are given.
2. Aaron Copland and Vivian Perlis, *Copland since 1943* (New York: St. Martin's Press, 1988), pp. 157-158.
3. Denis Donoghue, *Emily Dickinson* (University of Minnesota, 1969) p. 30.
4. Copland and Perlis, p. 438, notes 17 and 20.
5. Ibid., p. 159.
6. Donoghue, p. 14.
7. Wolff, p. 186.
8. Ibid., p. 128.
9. Copland and Perlis, p. 159.
10. R. B. Sewall, *The Life of Emily Dickinson*, Vol. II (New York: Farrar Strauss and Giroux, 1974) p. 547.
11. Poem #285, "The Buttercup's my whim for Bloom."
12. The curve of Dickinson's productivity, as far as it can be established, takes the following form: 1858—52 poems; 1859—94; 1860—64; 1861—86; 1862—366 (this extraordinary number may be the result of Dickinson's having made fair copies at this time of many poems actually written earlier; she was impelled to do this by the threat of blindness due to an eye ailment which peaked in 1862, only to recede and recur in later

years); 1863—141; 1864—174; 1865—85; 1866—36; from 1867 on—no more than 50 poems in any given year.

13. Copland and Perlis, p. 159.

14. Wolff. The term is used throughout the book. See, for example, discussions of "The Chariot" on p. 275 or of "I felt a Funeral in my Brain" on p. 227.

15. Copland and Perlis, p. 159.

16. Donoghue, p. 30.

17. Ibid., p. 221.

18. Wolff, See pp. 227-233 for a detailed analysis of the poem.

19. Ibid., pp. 118-119.

20. Ibid., p. 275.

21. Donoghue, p. 38.

BIBLIOGRAPHY

BOOKS

Auric, Georges, *Quand j'étais là...*, Grasset, 1979

Baudelaire, Charles, *Les Fleurs du mal et autre poèmes*, Garnier-Flammarion, 1964

Bernac, Pierre, *The Interpretation of French Song.* New York, Norton, 1978

Bornecque, Jacques-Henri. *Lumières sur les "Fêtes galantes" de Paul Verlaine.* Paris: Nizet, 1969.

_____. *Verlaine par lui-même.* Paris: Seuil, 1955

Brody, Elaine, and Fowkes, Robert, *The German Lied and its Poetry*, N. Y. U. Press, 1971

Brown, Calvin, *Music and Literature.* University of Georgia Press, 1948. rpt, 1963.

Carter, A. E. *Paul Verlaine.* New York: Twayne Pub., undated.

Coker, Wilson, *Music and Meaning.* New York: Free Press, 1972

Collingwood, R. G., *The Principles of Art.* Oxford University Press, 1938

Cone, Edward, *The Composer's Voice.* University of California Press, 1974

Copland, Aaron and Perlis, Vivian, *Copland since 1943.* New York: St. Martin's Press, 1989

Dalhaus, Carl, *Esthetics of Music*. Cambridge University, 1982

Deutsch, Babette, *Poetry Handbook*, 4th edition. Barnes and
    Noble, 1981

Donoghue, Denis, *Emily Dickinson*. Univ. of Minnesota, 1969

Epperson, Gordon, *The Musical Symbol*. Iowa State, 1967

Gautier, Théophile, *Pages choisies*. Classiques Larousse

Hall, J. H., *The Art Song*. Oklahoma: Norman Press, 1953

Hill, Edward, *Modern French Music*. New York: Houghton-
    Mifflin, 1924

Hollander, John, *Images of Voice*. Cambridge: Severs Ltd.,
    1970

Hospers, John, *Meaning and Truth in the Arts*. University of
    North Carolina, 1946

Ivey, Donald, *Song: Anatomy, Imagery, and Styles*. New York:
    Free Press, 1970

Kivy, Peter, *Reflections on Musical Expression*. Princeton
    University, 1980

Kramer, Lawrence, *Music and Poetry*. University of California,
    1984

Landormy, Paul, *La musique française de Franck à Debussy*.
    Paris: Gallimard, 1943

Langer, Susanne, *Feeling and Form*. New York: Scribner's,
    1953

_____. *Philosophy in a New Key*. Harvard University, 1957

Lesure, François, ed., *Claude Debussy: Critical Writings*.
Trans. R. L. Smith. New York: Knopf, 1977

Lukács, Georg, *Goethe and His Age*. Merlin Press, 1968,
trans. Robert Anchor

Major, Jean-Louis, *Radiguet-Cocteau "Les Joues en Feu"*. Univ.
of Ottowa Press, 1977

Mann, Thomas, *Doctor Faustus*. New York: Knopf, 1963

McNab, James, *Raymond Radiguet*. Twayne Pub. 1984

Meister, Barbara, *An Introduction to the Art Song*. New York:
Taplinger, 1980

____. *Nineteenth Century French Song*. Indiana University,
1980

Mellers, Wilfrid, *Man and His Music*. New York: Schocken,
1969

Menhennet, Alan, *Order and Freedom: Literature and Society
in Germany from 1790 to 1805*. New York: Basic
Books, 1973

Meyer, Leonard, *Emotion and Meaning in Music*. University of
Chicago, 1956

Miller, Philip, *The Ring of Words*. New York: Norton, 1973

Moser, Ruth, *L'impressionisme française*. Diss., Genève, 1951

Nadal, Octave, *Paul Verlaine*, Paris: Mercure de France, 1961

Penguin Book of German Verse, Intro. by Leonard Foster, 1959
ed. Richardson, Joanna, *Verlaine*. New York: Viking,
1971

Richer, Jean, *Paul Verlaine.* Paris: Seghers, 1960

Robertson, J. C., *A History of German Literature.* Fifth Ed., British Book Center, 1966

Rohozinski, L., ed., *Cinquante ans de musique française (1874-1925)* Tome II. Paris: Librairie de France

Rolland, Romain, *Musiciens d'aujourd'hui.* Paris: Librairie Hachette, 1922

Rorem, Ned, *Pure Contraption.* New York: Holt, Rinehart and Winston, 1974

Roz, Firmin, *La Littérature française.* Allyn and Bacon, 1945

Riwet, Nicolas, *Langage, musique, poésie.* Paris: Seuil, 1972

Sams, Eric, *The Songs of Hugo Wolf.* Eulenberg Books, 1972

Sartre, Jean Paul, *Mallarmé or the Poet of Nothingness.* trans. Ernest Sturm, Pennsylvania State Univ. Press, 1988

Sewall, R. B., *The Life of Emily Dickinson,* Vol II. New York: Farrar Straus and Giroux, 1974

Shattuck, Roger, *The Banquet Years: The Arts in France 1885-1918.* New York: Harcourt Brace, 1958

Stahl, E. L. and Yuill, W. E., *German Literature in the 18th and 19th Centuries.* Barnes and Noble, 1970

Stein, Jack, *Poem and Music in the German Lied.* Harvard Univ. Press, 1971

Steiner, George, *After Babel.* Oxford University, 1975

Stevens, Denis, *A History of Song.* New York: Norton, 1960

Suarès, André, *Debussy*. Paris: Emile-Paul frères, 1922

Tiersot, Julien, *Un demi-siècle de musique française: entre les deux guerres, 1870-1917*. Paris: Librairie Félix Alcan, 1918

Tovey, Sir Donald Francis, *Essays in Musical Analysis*, Vol. V. Oxford University Press, 1937

Vallas, Léon, *Claude Debussy: His Life and Works*. Trans. Maire and Grace O'Brien. New York: Dover, 1973

Verlaine, Paul, *Lettres inédites à divers correspondants*. ed. Georges Zayed. Genève: 1976

____. *Oeuvres en prose complètes*. Jacques Borel, ed., Paris: Gallimard.

____. *Oeuvres poétiques*. Jacques Robichez, ed. Paris: Garnier, 1969

Weaver, William and Chusid, Martin, eds., *The Verdi Companion*. Norton, 1979

Wenk, Arthur, *Debussy and the Poets*. Univ. of California, 1976

Winn, James Anderson, *Unsuspected Eloquence*. Yale Univ. Press, 1981

Wolff, Cynthia Griffin, *Emily Dickinson*. New York: Knopf, 1986

Zayed, Georges, *La formation littéraire de Verlaine*. Paris: Librairie Nizet, 1970

Zimmerman, Eléonore, *Les magies de Verlaine*. Paris: José Corti, 1967

ARTICLES

Auric, Georges, article in *La Nouvelle Revue française*, Feb.
    1921

Barzun, Jacques, "Music Into Words." in *Score* #10, Dec. 1954.
    London, Score Pub.

Berthelot, R. "Défense de la poésie chantée." in *La Revue
    musicale* #19, July-December 1938. Paris: La Revue
    Musicale Pub.

Brown, Calvin, "The Poetic Use of Musical Form." in *Musical
    Quarterly*, XXX. 1944. New York: Macmillan

Carco, Francis, "Verlaine." in *Nouvelle revue critique.* Paris:
    1938

Castelnuovo-Tedesco, Mario, "Music and Poetry: Problems of
    a Song Writer." in *Musical Quarterly*, XXX. 1944.
    New York: Macmillan

Cocteau, Jean, article in *Le Coq et l'Arlequin.* 1919

Cone, Edward, "Schubert's Promissory Note." in *Nineteenth
    Century Music*, Spring, 1982

Cuénot, C. "La situation de Paul Verlaine," in *Information
    littéraire*, mars-juin, 1957. Paris: Société d'Editions
    de Belles Lettres

Frye, Northrop, "Sound and Poetry." in English Institute
    Essays. Columbia University, 1956

Hollander, John, "The Music of Poetry," in *Journal of
    Aesthetics and Art Criticism*, Vol 15, 1956-7

Leclerc, T. "Les musiciens de Verlaine," in *La revue bleu*
    1903, Paris: Dir. Félix du Moulin

Newcomb, Anthony, "Sound and Feeling." in *Critical Inquiry*,
    June 1984. University of Chicago Press

Nichols, Roger, "Debussy's Two Settings of 'Clair de Lune.'"
    in *Music and Letters*, #48, 1967. Oxford University
    Press

Noakes, David, critique of "Alphabet" in *La Larousse mensuel*
    of January 1925

Oliphant, E. "Poetry and the Composer," in *Musical Quart-
    erly*, April, 1922. New York: Macmillan

La Revue musicale #7. Mai-octobre, 1926. Paris: Editions
    Richard Masse. (Issue devoted to Debussy)